Faster than a speeding tod
More powerful than a corpora
Able to leap over mountains of laundry i
Supermom?

No—She's a WORK-AT-HOME MOM!

ARE YOU A WAHM?

When you drive to work, do you think:

A. Phew, I'm glad to get away from my family.

B. I'm sure the socialization at child care is good for my children.

C. I can't do this anymore.

The laundry and dirty dishes are piled up, you have a job deadline looming. You:

A. Drop everything and clean, clean, clean.

B. Try to finish the job, but you just can't concentrate until the dishes are done.

C. Finish the job; the dishes will still be there when you're done.

When you see a successful businesswoman, do you think:

A. I am so jealous of her.

B. Why is she wearing those shoes with that dress?

C. I could do that!

Note: If you answered "c" to all the above questions, you might just have what it takes to be a Work-At-Home Mom. And if you already are a WAHM, this book has the support and encouragement you need to stay in business—and stay sane!

It's a Jungle Out There and a Zoo in Here

Run Your Home Business without Letting It Overrun You

*

Cheryl Demas

WARNER BOOKS

An AOL Time Warner Company

Warner Books, Inc., 1271 Avenue of the Americas, New York, NY 10020

Visit our Web site at www.twbookmark.com

An AOL Time Warner Company

Printed in the United States of America

First Printing: May 2003

10   9   8   7   6   5   4   3   2   1

Library of Congress Cataloging-in-Publication Data

Demas, Cheryl.
    It's a jungle out there and a zoo in here : run your home business without letting it overrun you / Cheryl Demas.
        p. cm.
    Includes bibliographical references and index.
    ISBN 0-446-67972-0
    1. Home-based businesses—Planning. 2. Women-owned business enterprises—Management. 3. New business enterprises—Management. I. Title.
    HD62.38 .D46 2003
    658'.041—dc21

                                                                        2002031142

Book design by Nancy Singer Olaguera
Cover design by Brigid Pearson
Cover illustration by Phillip Brooker

For Mike, Nicki, and Dani

What would I do without you?

Acknowledgments

There are so many people to thank for their help with this book. First of all, Elizabeth Kanna for introducing me to the people at Warner Books. My dream editor, Molly Chehak, who has been such a pleasure to work with. Everyone else at Warner Books, Laura Jorstad, Nancy Singer Olaguera, Eric Wechter, they're a great team.

My husband, Mike, for being my biggest fan and for his willingness to do anything for me at anytime. My girls, Nicki and Dani, for helping me with ideas and for listening to my stories over and over again. Everyone else in our extended family for their support and encouragement.

Special thanks to all of the work-at-home moms, my online friends and e-mail buddies who contributed their ideas and advice for this book. I can't name you all, but I appreciate your input and I'm thankful for your friendship.

Contents

Introduction

We all know what Tarzan said to his wife every night when he came home from work.

"Jane, it's a jungle out there."

And Tarzan wasn't even dealing with pumps, panty hose, and pacifiers.

Yes, it's a jungle—especially for working moms. I know; I was there.

No matter how family friendly a workplace claims to be, it is always expected, or at least hoped, that the company will be first in your life. Your children and your family life have to be worked into your work schedule. That's the reality of life in the third millennium.

In the fifties moms were expected to be perfect homemakers. In the seventies we were expected to have thriving careers and leave the homemaking to someone else. Now moms are expected to both manage a career and be perfect homemakers. Is that progress? I don't think so.

I didn't always feel this way. If you had told the twenty-two-year-old me, "Cheryl, in twenty years you will have quit your job to stay home with your kids and be a mom," twenty-two-year-old Cheryl would have laughed in your face. I cheered when Billy Jean King beat

Bobby Riggs. I sang along with "I Am Woman, Hear Me Roar." I wasn't going to be a housewife, for heaven's sake.

When Warner Books decided it was time to publish a comprehensive advice book for the work-at-home mom, they set out in search of a woman who could lead by example. They were looking for a woman who lives in an immaculate house, runs a successful home business, and has a vibrant marriage and happy, well-adjusted children. A woman who has it all together. Unable to find such a woman, they asked me to write this book.

Of course I agreed, not because I think I have all the answers, but because I know so many of you have questions. I hear from hundreds of you every day, through the e-mails and messages I get from my Web site, WAHM.com—The Online Magazine for Work-at-Home Moms. I believe I have found at least some of the answers (and most of the questions).

I hope you find a few laughs here, maybe a few things that make you think. Working at home may not be for everyone, and it isn't always easy, but it certainly has been worth it for me. If you're in the traditional workplace, and if you're happy with that, good for you. I'm not here to change your mind. But if you're wondering if there's a better way, if you wish you could stay home, I want you to know that you're not alone.

This book is for those of you who are tired of the juggling act and the traditional workplace. If you're ready to make a change, it's time to get started. Thinking about it, waiting, and wishing aren't going to make anything happen. It's time to take action, and this is the place to start. I will give you a step-by-step plan to help you prepare your budget, decide if working at home is right for you, choose a business, get your business started, and make it a success. I hope you will read this book as you start your business and return to it from time to time as your business grows. Pick it up when you need support or when you need to reaffirm your decision to work at home. It can be done; thousands of women are doing it already, and you can be the next success story.

Now that I've been working at home for about seven years, I know that I've made the right decision. I love being home with my girls and I can't imagine a "traditional" job that would give me the satisfaction I get from raising them. The good news is that motherhood isn't a one-way street. I'm getting back so much more from my role as mom than I'm giving. I know people always say that being a parent is the most difficult job there is, and there *are* challenges, but I can't imagine anything else I'd rather be doing. I really believe I have the best of both worlds.

My younger daughter summed it up for me as she was getting ready for bed one night. She asked me, "Mom, what would you do without me?" I thought about our bedtime stories, hugs, "I love Mommy" notes, and the laughs we have together. That night, as I watched her sleep, I thought the same thing myself: What would I do without them?

I never saw myself as a stay-at-home mom, but that is what I've become. A stay-at-home mom with a twist—I'm now a work-at-home mom. Like millions of women, I've combined a home business with my "housewife" role and now have what I believe to be the best of both worlds. I'm home with my kids and I'm still working. What could be better than that? Staying at home with my kids isn't a sacrifice for me; it is a joy. Sure, I still have other interests and things I like to do that don't include the kids—my home business, for example. But nothing is more important to me than being here for my children. I wouldn't trade these days for anything; money, status, titles— none of it means as much to me as my main title, Mom. And judging by the number of visitors to WAHM.com and the mail I receive, there are a lot of other moms who agree.

The Jungle

My Life as a Working Mother

In between cheering for Billy Jean King and singing "I Am Woman," I went to college and graduated with a double major in math and computer science. In keeping with my feminist life course, I had chosen two of the more nontraditional female courses of study that I could find. However, I do have to admit that I had also calculated that I would find the most favorable boy/girl ratio in my math classes. How's that for sisterhood?

After graduation, I went to work in the avionics department of a large computer company. My main job while there was modeling—no, not like Cindy Crawford—I did mathematical modeling of pressure transducers. The avionics group produced computers that are used on airplanes—you know, those black boxes you always hear about. Each transducer had slightly different characteristics over pressure and temperature ranges, so the flight computers were programmed to adjust for these differences. My job was to write software that would "fit" each transducer with an equation that matched its output. To collect data on each unit, we would run them through temperatures from minus forty degrees Fahrenheit to about two hundred degrees in huge industrial ovens. It was probably my most productive kitchen work to date.

I met my future husband my first week of work. I had had orthodontic surgery a few weeks before I started my new job, so my jaw was wired shut and I could only nod and smile.

I was his dream girl.

By the time the wires came out and I could talk again, it was too late. We were in love. We were married the following year. We knew we wanted children right away, maybe two or three. I got pregnant and expected to continue working through my pregnancy and then search for day care. I honestly didn't think that I would even consider staying at home. I remember my mom saying to me, "Well *of course* you'll want to stay home with your babies." And I remember looking at her as if she had sprouted horns.

But life had different plans for us.

My mother died of breast cancer that summer. When things were looking particularly bad for Mom, her doctor gave her some alternatives. She could cease treatment altogether, or they could do more surgery and extend her life for a short while longer, but the cancer had gone beyond any hope for a cure.

"Could you keep me alive long enough to see the baby, until October?" she asked the doctor.

The answer was no, and so with that prognosis, my mom decided that her fight was over. She died June 30. I was six months pregnant and at her side when she died. "You are going to be the best mom in the world" were among her last words to me.

A couple months later I went into labor. It was a little early, but my obstetrician didn't seem to be too concerned, even when she observed that the baby was breech. Everything switched into high gear. The staff became quiet and efficient, prepped me for surgery, and wheeled me in for an emergency C-section. Just before they put me under, the nurse asked, "What would you like us to tell your baby when he gets here?"

"Just tell him to be healthy," I answered.

Mike arrived at the hospital just after the birth. He was armed with his video camera, ready to tape those first precious moments. The nurses met him in the hall with bad news. Our baby boy had just been born and he was going to die. There was nothing they could do to save him. His condition was what the medical community calls "incompatible with life."

There are times in life that you can't possibly be prepared for. The death of a baby is one of those times. They put Mike in scrubs and brought him into the delivery room. I was still under anesthesia, so he was alone. The nurses asked if he wanted to baptize the baby. He did, but we had decided to wait until we saw our baby before we made a final decision on his name. Since I was still asleep, Mike didn't want to make that decision without me. The nurses brought him a bowl of water and Mike baptized our baby, saying that we didn't have a name picked out for him yet but that God would know him when he got there.

I was awake by then and the doctor told me the news. I closed my eyes and tried to go back to sleep. It had to be a dream.

"I don't think she heard you," the nurse said, "tell her again."

So it wasn't a dream.

"No, I heard."

Mike was holding our son, and I got a chance to hold him too before he died. Looking at his precious face and not being able to do anything for him was the hardest thing I've ever done. I was his mom. Aren't moms supposed to fix everything for their kids? Here I was, a brand-new mom, and I was already screwing up.

The nurses took Polaroids, our minister arrived, we held our baby a little longer, and then they took our son away. I guess my mom got to take care of her grandson after all.

Now, even on the craziest days, when the house is a wreck and I have way too much to do, I think back to that day. Having held my son as he drew his last breaths, it's pretty hard to get upset about crumbs in the car or fingerprint smudges on the windows.

I got pregnant again after several months, and at the end of a stressful, anxious pregnancy, our daughter Nicole was born. She was perfect and healthy. I knew then, after all we had been through to have her, that I didn't want to leave her to go back to work. But I didn't want to quit working either, so I started searching for alternatives. At first my husband and I worked split shifts, and then I did contract engineering work from home for my old employer. I hadn't quite reconciled myself to the idea that I might just quit work. I felt that I had invested so much in my education and career; I didn't want to just walk away from it all. But even with all our creative scheduling and solutions, I always felt torn. I liked working, and we enjoyed the things we could do with the extra income. But when we worked split shifts, my husband and I hardly ever saw each other, meeting just for a short baby handoff. I felt that neither one of us could completely devote ourselves to our careers, and we were always having to make compromises. When the baby was sick, one of us would take time off. Working overtime was out of the question. We were viewed at work as not being completely devoted to the company, and we couldn't completely devote ourselves to our home lives either. Mike's boss (who had a stay-at-home wife) even commented that he knew he couldn't count on Mike to do after-hours projects because Mike "always had to run off to day care."

When Nicki was about three, I returned to work full-time. Even after everything we had been through, I couldn't become "just" a mom. Whenever I thought about staying home, I could hear Helen Reddy and Billie Jean King in the back of my mind saying "After all we've done for you, this is the thanks we get?" I read all the books, the articles, the magazines; I watched the TV interviews. If other working mothers were successfully "having it all," then I wanted to have it all too. So we hired a nanny—she was a friend of the family and Nicki loved her. We then licensed our home for child care, and our nanny took care of a couple neighborhood children too. Nicki got to stay home every day, and she had her friends over every day to play too. But I still wasn't happy with someone other than me taking care of my daughter for the majority of her waking hours. We continued to try to have another child, but after more losses, a total of six pregnancies and only one living child, we just couldn't do it anymore. We decided that Nicki would be an only child.

In 1992 my husband got a job offer that moved us from Minnesota to California. Nicki started kindergarten that year, and then I found a job with a software company. With Nicki in school, I assumed that fitting a full-time work schedule into our daily routines would be easier. It wasn't. There were still sick days, school holidays—tons of school holidays—business trips. I learned the language of school calendars, minimum days, superminimum days, supersecret minimum days. It took a personal computer just to keep track of when I was supposed to do drop-offs and pickups. The stress of it all was hard on the three of us, and still neither Mike nor I could fully devote ourselves to either our careers or the family. We searched for balance, but it was elusive. Nicki was growing up so quickly, and I was sad that I was still missing so much of her life.

Living in California gave us a new appreciation for the natural lifestyle, and we decided to forgo chemical birth control in favor of a more natural calendar-watching method, using condoms during the "danger days." I decided I'd just pick some up where I always shop—the warehouse shopping club. Of course, one can't buy just one or two of anything at the warehouse store, so my only choice was a case of condoms. Twelve boxes, 12 condoms in each . . . sounded about right to me! The young cashier couldn't believe I was buying 144 condoms and set them aside until everything else had been rung up.

She held them up high for the entire line behind me to see and said, "These aren't—*like*—yours, are they?"

Yes, you little vixen, they were indeed mine.

But I might as well have—*like*—given them to her, because a month later I was pregnant again. And after an anxious nine months, we prepared to deliver another beautiful, healthy little girl. I investigated the maternity policy at my new job and we checked out local child-care alternatives. We were so far away from our old friends and family, and I couldn't imagine leaving my new baby with a stranger. Maybe this time I would stay home for good.

But even though Mike had a good job, we had set up our household budget based on two incomes, and given the cost of living in California, it was difficult to see how we could possibly get by on just one. We put the decision on hold and agreed that we would decide for sure one way or another after the baby was born.

Then the roller coaster began again. I had a C-section scheduled for a Friday morning, and Mike had to go out of town for work, but he was due to return Thursday. My mother-in-law was arriving from Florida on Wednesday.

Now, I love my mother-in-law as much as the next woman, but we are about as different as we can be. She is an old-world Greek mom—she takes great pride in caring for her family, and she's great at it. When she's visiting us, all Mike has to do is clear his throat and she leaps to her feet to get him a glass of water. His tummy rumbles and she's preparing a five-course meal. The two words I hear most often when she stays with us are "Poor Mike."

As usual, I had planned on transforming myself into a whirlwind cleaning machine the day before she arrived. So when I would normally have cleaned the bathroom on Saturday, I figured I'd leave it and clean everything on Tuesday. Then the whole house would be really fresh and clean on Wednesday when she arrived. Right? Wrong.

Nicki had a softball game that Monday night and she just wasn't herself. It was an incredibly hot day, so her extreme thirst didn't seem that unusual. But she had to go to the bathroom so often—before her softball game, during the third and fifth innings, and again after the game. Now, that was unusual.

My hypochondriac hobby was about to pay off. The late nights I'd spent reading over symptoms and diseases would finally be put to use. Extreme thirst and frequent urination sounded like diabetes to me. I stopped at the drugstore on our way home from the game and picked up some test strips that would check for sugar in her urine.

Positive.

I called the doctor and was advised to bring her in to the office the next morning to confirm the test. Again, positive. "Go home and pack a bag, then go straight to the hospital," I was told. "She will have to be admitted, and she'll be there about a week."

"But—I'm going to have a baby on Friday—I have to clean today!" I wanted to say. The doctor didn't care, and of course I knew that we had no choice. Nicki had to be hospitalized, and our lives would never be the same. Just how much they would change, I had no idea.

What a week that was. I spent the last three nights of my pregnancy sleeping in a chair at Nicki's bedside. The whole family had to learn how to draw up insulin, give shots, and prick her little fingers for blood tests. We had to learn the complicated system of keeping her blood sugar in normal ranges: how to balance her diet, activity, and insulin, and walk the tightrope between high and low blood sugar—the routine that would be part of our lives from then on. Nicki did so well that her doctor agreed to release her from the hospital on Friday.

Of course our baby wasn't being delivered at the same hospital— that would have been too convenient. So before dawn on Friday morning, Mike and his mom came to the hospital, his mom stayed with Nicki, we drove back across town, had a baby, Mike drove back to get Nicki and his mom, and they all came back across town to meet our newest family member, Danielle. Nicki wasn't used to any-one but me giving her shots or doing her blood tests, so I was motivated to get home as soon as possible. Even after the C-section I was up and around the first night, and we were all home again by Sunday morning. I knew then that there was no way I would be able to go back to work. The decision had been made for us—I would stay home with the girls. I was determined to make "mom" my number one job. I was needed at home, and home is where I wanted to be. Nicki was going to be all right. We would all be all right, I would see to it.

I had just one nagging question in the back of my mind. How would we pay the bills?

2

Me Tarzan, You Jane, We Broke

Can You Afford to Stay Home?

I knew that I wanted to stay home with my girls more than any-thing, yet I still had concerns. Would I be bored at home? Would I miss the chats with my coworkers? And most important, how could we get along with just one paycheck?

Ideally we would have adjusted our budget before I quit my job—better yet, before I even got pregnant. But since my stay-at-home decision was spontaneous and somewhat emotional, my advice is to do as I say, not as I did.

Living frugally has never been a strength of mine. I can't bring myself to wash and reuse my plastic bags or make Christmas orna-ments out of recycled panty hose. But we tried. We canceled cable, we had one car, we didn't take any vacations, we didn't eat out. And we got by. It was tight sometimes, but we made it.

If you're contemplating leaving your job to stay at home, you must first work on your budget. Sit down and really look at where your money goes now and what expenses you could eliminate, and assess whether or not you can make it work. If you can't see how you will be able to quit working right away, make a plan. Maybe start your home business part-time at first and give it a chance to start generating some income before you make the big leap to staying home full-time.

I soon discovered many online resources and books that helped me cut back on expenses. One of my favorites was a book of recipes I found for homemade Christmas gifts. "Nothing says love like something from your kitchen," it told me. My kitchen? Really? I decided to give it a try. A particular recipe for a homemade coffee liqueur intrigued me, so I went to the grocery store to pick up the ingredients. When I went to the checkout, the contents of my cart consisted of two pounds of coffee and a fifth of vodka.

"Looks like this was an emergency trip," the clerk said with a smirk as he rang up the sale. The gifts never really turned out, but I had fun experimenting with the recipe.

Even though that didn't work out very well, I didn't give up on economizing.

When we had a power crisis here in California recently, I strung a rope across our back deck, which served as an old-fashioned clothesline. I bought a bag of clothespins and I was in business.

My teenage daughter came home just as I was hanging up my first load of wet clothes. She was mortified. "Mother! Come in here right now. What do you think you're doing? Haven't you heard? This is the twenty-first century, you know."

"Nicki," I answered, "it's simple, it's natural, and it's solar powered. Haven't you heard? There's an energy crisis, you know."

"But do you have to do this out here where everyone can see you?"

"Well, it's kind of hard to hang clothes outside without actually going outdoors."

She just rolled her eyes and walked away. At the very least, I was fulfilling my duty of embarrassing my daughter.

I also discovered the many services that are available at no cost in our community. For example, we use the public library a lot. Do you realize how much you can get for free at the library? We check out books on tape and videos; we read magazines—it's a terrific resource. We attend story times at the local bookstores, and we go on field trips with other moms to candy shops, the grocery store—we see all the behind-the-scenes action that is usually off-limits to the public. We also discovered how much fun it was to just pack up a simple picnic and spend the day at the park. I love the freedom of being able to schedule my day and plan our outings. An annual pass to our local zoo turned out to be a great investment. We have really gotten to know those animals.

We found other ways to have cheap fun. Boxes are amazing—don't kids always play with the box more than the toy anyway? We saved a step and just brought home the box. Grocery stores, warehouse clubs—they're all great sources of boxes. Just ask; they will save them for you. With the addition of some black and white squares of paper, a huge box became a giant game board. I put the kids to work fashioning game pieces from ordinary household items. One time they made an entire chess set out of juice boxes and soda bottles. We built a geodesic dome out of rolled-up newspapers; we applied papier-mâché to anything that wasn't moving.

We squeezed the budget as tight as we could, and sometimes, even now, cash doesn't exactly flow. During those times we impose zero-tolerance spending days. The girls know that there's no sense in even asking for something during one of those times. My girls still talk about the days of "the spending freeze," as we called it, like the old folks in Minnesota talk about the Armistice Day blizzard. They'll get quiet and serious, speaking in hushed tones. "Remember the spending freeze?" one will say. The other will nod silently, as if invoking its name might cause it to reappear.

It's Too Cold for Belly Dancing

On *really* cold days back in Minnesota, the fuel line in Mike's car would literally freeze while he was driving. He called me one night as I was waiting for him to come home. His car had broken down again, he was stranded far from home, and the temperature was twenty degrees below zero. But he didn't sound as miserable as I thought he should. He had walked to the nearest restaurant and called me while he waited for the tow truck. Well . . . not exactly the *closest* restaurant. I wondered why I heard music and jingling in the background. As luck would have it, the car had broken down within walking distance of a restaurant that featured belly dancing during happy hour.

So, maybe being stranded in twenty-below weather wasn't Mike's idea of a good time, but he managed to find a way to make the most of it. You can always find a way to make the most of your situation too. Try not to focus on the lack of money but on the positive lessons you can teach your kids as you manage your budget. There's always a bright side.

Here are some more ways to put a positive spin on your cost-cutting activities.

You'll save money when you:	The added benefit is:
Stop eating out	You can eat healthier meals and have more control over what your family eats.
Own just one car	You can drive your husband to work when you need the car and spend more time together. You'll also get exercise if you walk more.
Cancel cable TV	You can spend more quality time with your family, playing board games, taking walks, and reading books.
Stop using credit cards	You won't be as tempted to make impulse purchases that you'll regret later.
Make homemade gifts and greeting cards	Relatives will appreciate the time you've devoted to them, and grandparents usually prefer items made by their grandchildren anyway.

You'll save money when you:	The added benefit is:
Plant a garden	You'll eat more vegetables.
Join a babysitting co-op	You and your children will meet new friends.

Remember that there are also many expenses associated with working away from home that can be eliminated when one parent is home full-time.

You won't have to spend as much on panty hose and a business wardrobe. If you won't be out meeting with clients, you will be able to work in jeans and sweatshirts most of the time. If you often bought fast-food meals because you were always running behind

when you were working away from home, you will find that cooking at home can be another great money saver. Child care is probably the biggest expense that will be eliminated when you leave the traditional workplace. However, depending on what type of job you choose and the ages of your children, you still might need to plan for some supplementary child care. Commuting costs are, of course, saved.

Over the years, I've met some champion frugal moms. Jenny Wanderscheid, the owner and founder of ChildFun.com, was particularly low on money when she decided that she needed to purchase her own domain name. Her husband supported her business, but they had absolutely no room in their budget for any additional expenses, so she knew her husband wouldn't agree to spend money on a domain purchase. Then Jenny remembered the blood center in her town, so she drove down and sold her plasma. That gave her the seventy dollars she needed and ChildFun.com was hers. Her site was literally started with blood money.

Another work-at-home mom sent me an e-mail asking if I could verify a rumor she had heard. According to the rumor, there is a clinic somewhere that will pay fifty thousand dollars for a testicle. How would you like to sit in on that family meeting? "Honey? You know how we're getting behind on our bills? Well . . . I think I've found a solution."

Of course, there are two sides to every equation. Spend less and/or earn more. Since spending less was only getting us so far, I decided to search for a way to make more money.

And please, before you do anything desperate, make sure you've done everything possible to reduce your expenses and maximize your income. Although I have been thinking: If we could get fifty thousand dollars for one testicle, I wonder what they'd give us for the "whole package"?

THE HILLSIDE POOL

Lately we have been talking about putting a swimming pool in our backyard. But putting in a pool would mean that we would have to take out my daughter's swing set, which she's not too happy about. She's slowly come around to agree that we would have a lot of fun with the pool, but there's just one little detail she can't quite figure out. The other day she asked me, "Mom, if we do put a pool in the backyard, how are we going to keep the water in it?" I went into a long explanation about evaporation, and how it's a slow process, and that they make systems that keep the water level of the pool constant, blah, blah, blah.

"No, no, no," she finally said, "I mean, our backyard is on a hill. How will we keep the water from rolling out?"

Our budget sometimes feels like that too. We bring our paychecks home, and it all rolls out again. Examine this factor carefully when you're setting up your budget and choosing your business. Be aware of where your money is going; watch every expenditure. You might not think that daily cup of coffee is that expensive, but even $2 a day adds up to $730 a year. When I realized that my habit of stopping for coffee at the coffee shop was really adding up to a big expense, I bought a box of cups and lids at the warehouse store, and now I make coffee for myself before I leave home. I still have the feeling of "special" coffee, but it's a lot cheaper.

If you're considering starting a direct-sales business, beware of businesses that require you to buy a large amount of overpriced merchandise to remain active with the company and pressure you to recruit new salespeople. It may be that the company makes its money off sales to the representatives, not from retail sales.

Be careful, too, that you're not your own best customer. When I was little, I remember asking my mom why the doughnut man was *so* large. She said he was "eating all the profits." I wondered what a

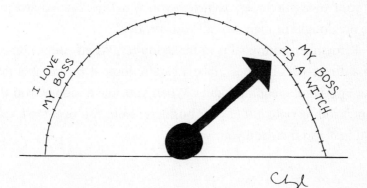

MOOD METER

FOR THE

SELF-EMPLOYED

I LOVE MY BOSS · MY BOSS IS A WITCH

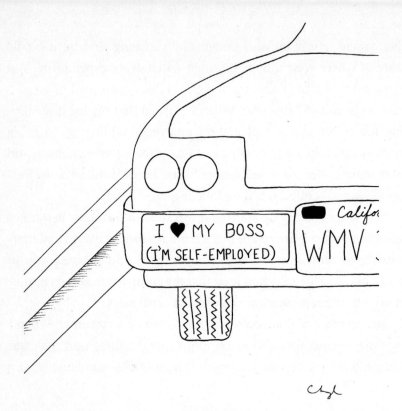

profit was and why he would want to eat so many. If you own a business that sells products, keep track of your personal purchases. If you like the products, allow yourself a certain percentage of your profits for your own purchases. That way you won't get carried away and, like my doughnut man, "eat all your profits."

Remember, your goal is to make money. When you're considering a direct-sales business, take a careful look at the compensation plan and your spending habits. When you make money, you don't want it rolling right out of your business again. You've got to level the land first and then add your water.

PROBLEM
I can't afford to quit my job to start a home business.

SOLUTIONS FROM SISTER ZOOS
Take a look at things that you can do without. Little things can add up to a lot of money. Stop eating out and renting movies, and start shopping garage sales for kids' clothes.

Nancy C., Minnesota

Get thrifty. Buy a six-pack of soft drinks on sale for $1.49 instead of paying a dollar apiece for each one, or stop drinking soda altogether. Cut out pizza night for a while, and clean out your storage areas and sell a few things on eBay or have a garage sale (this will also give you more space for your home office).

Lynn T., Tennessee

I save money by shopping at warehouse stores and staying out of the regular grocery stores unless I need a specialty item. Bulk shopping saves tons of money. We rarely eat out. I make everything from scratch, including pizza. It's much better than frozen or delivery. My husband gets the leftovers for lunches. I rarely, if ever, buy premade, preservative-laden frozen foods. We also wait a couple of weeks longer between haircuts, and the savings really add up.

Leslie, New Mexico

Balance your wants and needs. Now I ask myself, "Do I really need this?" before I buy anything, and the answer is usually no. Sure, I *want* a lot of stuff, but I don't *need* much. I have some friends who spend money like crazy and then tell me, "I'd love to stay home, but I have to work." What they're really saying is, "I want this stuff more than I want to stay home."

Jenny P., Texas

Leaving your outside job is scary; even when you should be ready to leave you'll resist . . . it's the fear factor working here. Sometimes you just have to "close your eyes and jump!"

Denise C., Rhode Island

You can test the waters for your home business while you are still working outside the home, bringing in steady income. Choose a business that you can work part-time and around your schedule. Start off slow and work up to where you'd like to be. I started my book-selling home business four years ago while working a full-time job. At first I just worked on it two times per month, then once a week. After two years, I quit working outside the home altogether and transitioned into work-at-home motherhood.

Kassandra T., Arizona

Weekends are built for this! I know thousands of people who start businesses with full-time jobs. It's just a matter of organizing your time off to do what you love.

Calissa L., Florida

Start slowly in your spare time so that you don't have to quit. Work on your marketing plan, identify your target market, price supplies, and find out who your competition is while you're still working full-time. When you've acquired a few customers, work on a budget so you know what your profits versus losses will look like. When your net income equals your take-home pay, then you can think about quitting!

Mia C., Wisconsin

I decided when I lost my job that it was time to start my home business, so the decision was made for me.

Beth T., New Hampshire

Don't quit your job. Consider negotiating with your current employer to continue some of your work from home as an employee. This will require flexibility on his or her part and accountability on yours. Working at home can save you money on commuting and day care and saves the employer money on overhead and office space. Of course, this will take a lot of organization and self-motivation, but it can pay off in the end.

Tricia T.

HOME BUSINESS PROBLEM #57

THE CORPORATE CAFETERIA IS ALWAYS OPEN

Start your business part-time at first, maybe working nights and weekends. At first you may feel like you are working two jobs, when the idea was to spend more time at home with your family, but in the end you will be able to establish your business without losing the income. Cut back to part-time expenses so that if you launch full-time or quit the day job, you will be used to a tighter budget. Put away the other "half" of the income, or use it to start your business.

April G., Washington

I have started using coupons this past year. Many people say they don't have time, but I have seen for myself that I save a lot of money at the grocery store. The trick is having coupons to use on the same items the store has on sale. And go to a store that doubles coupons. I ask my neighbors and family members to save their Sunday coupons for me. Most don't clip them and they are more than happy to give them to me. I've gotten one hundred dollars' worth of groceries for sixty dollars because of coupons.

Theresa G., California

Start your business while you're still working your other job— work nights and weekends if need be to root the new venture. If you don't have the time or drive to do this—maybe you're looking at the wrong home business, or perhaps working at home isn't right for you.

Nancy P., California

Now that you have your budget under control, it's time to decide if working at home is right for you.

3

Now You Know You Can Swing It

Is It Really for You?

Next you need to determine if working at home is right for you. Perhaps you know that you could use the extra money, but maybe you're not sure if you have what it takes to work on your own. I came up with this little quiz to help any of you who might be unsure. Imagine yourself in the following situations and pick the item that most closely describes your response:

1. You inherit one thousand dollars from a long-lost relative. You think:
   A. Great! Now I can take that vacation I've always dreamed of.
   B. I could sure use a new wardrobe.
   C. Woo-hoo! Now I can buy a laser printer!

2. You get a new computer; now you can:
   A. Finally get your recipes organized.
   B. Learn to play one of those multiplayer Internet games.
   C. Set up your business Web site.

3. The laundry and dirty dishes are piled up, you have a job dead-line looming, and you:
   A. Drop everything and clean, clean, clean.
   B. Try to finish the job, but you just can't concentrate until the dishes are done.
   C. Finish the job; the dishes will still be there when you're done.

4. It's 1:00 A.M.; you are most happy if you are:
   A. Sleeping.
   B. Out on the town.
   C. Preparing invoices.

5. When you see a successful businesswoman, you think:
   A. I am so jealous of her.
   B. Why is she wearing those shoes with that dress?
   C. I could do that!

6. When you drive into work, you think:
   A. Phew, I'm glad to get away from my family.
   B. I'm sure the socialization at child care is good for my children.
   C. I can't do this anymore.

If you answered "C" to all the above questions, congratulations! I'd say you have what it takes to be a work-at-home mom. (*Author's Note:* If anyone chose "A" on question no. 3, I'd like to give you my address because I could really use someone like you at my house.)

WHICH MOM HAS A HOME BUSINESS ?

WHAT DOES IT TAKE?

If you're thinking you might like to start a home business but aren't sure if your personality is right for the work-at-home lifestyle, I have good news. I've met an amazingly large variety of people through my Web site. There are work-at-home moms all over the world, doing every imaginable type of work at home. They live in big cities and in rural areas. There are married WAHMs, single WAHMs, and Grandma WAHMs. They are all successful work-at-home moms, and they use the strengths of their different personality styles to their advantage. But even with all the diversity, successful WAHMs seem to have a few things in common.

Entrepreneurial Spirit

The typical WAHM has a strong entrepreneurial personality. She may have been the first child in her neighborhood to set up a lemonade stand in the summer or organize a used-toy sale with her friends. She is always looking for a new way to make money. She is energized by the idea of starting something from scratch and thrives on the excitement of a new business venture.

Resilience

The successful WAHM knows that ups and downs are part of doing business and she doesn't let the bad times keep her down for long. Although she knows enough to cut her losses and move on when it becomes apparent that a particular venture isn't going to work out, she doesn't let a setback keep her from pursuing her work-at-home dreams. So even if her first attempts at a home business don't live up to her expectations, she perseveres and keeps trying. Shari Fitzpatrick, founder of Shari's Berries, learned this lesson early in her business. When she first started her strawberry-dipping business, she was working from her home kitchen. It's fine to run the paperwork side of a food business from home, but the actual food preparation has to be done from a commercial kitchen. One day Shari received an anonymous phone call warning her that a competitor had turned her in to the health department. Hours later, an inspector was knocking on her door. Thanks to the phone call, she was prepared. She had pulled her blinds and didn't answer the door. Then she quickly arranged to sublease kitchen space from a friend who owned a commercial kitchen. The next day she was able to invite the inspector to come with her to her commercial kitchen, where she did all her strawberry dipping. Now Shari says that she knows that when something bad happens, as long as she learns something from it that will prevent it from happening again, it's not such a bad thing. She looks at it as a learning experience that will help her in the future, when making the mistake again would be even more detrimental. What threatened to be a horrible setback at the time gave her the nudge she needed to move into commercial space. Now she's thankful for that nudge. Her company's revenues grew from six hundred thousand dollars to more than seven million dollars in three years, and she has sold more than one and a half million berries, dipped in thirty-six tons of chocolate, to more than seventy-five thousand customers in the last twelve months alone.

Dedication

Dedication to her business is another trait of a successful WAHM. She is a hard worker and is willing to go the extra mile to make her business stand out from the rest. If it means late nights and early mornings or carrying samples in and out of demonstrations, she is willing to do whatever it takes. She is dedicated to her business, and she keeps working to make it a success.

Creativity

The typical WAHM is creative. She sees a business opportunity around every corner. Since she doesn't have a lot of role models for her work-at-home lifestyle, she has to be creative to adapt her schedule and environment to her unique situation and to the changing needs of her business and family.

Independence

WAHMs are independent. The typical WAHM is able to work on her own, and she has the self-discipline needed to meet deadlines and work when no one is standing over her.

Realistic Attitude

The successful WAHM may have big goals and dreams, but she also has a realistic vision of what she will be able to accomplish with her home businesses. She looks at the time and resources she has available and makes a realistic plan.

Desire

Last but not least, the typical WAHM has a strong desire to work at home. She knows that she wants to be at home and take care of her children, yet she still wants to work and make money. She is motivated to succeed, and she has faith in herself.

Brenda Hyde, publisher and founder of OldFashionedLiving.com, says, "I would never return to the traditional workplace. It's not just staying home with the kids. I feel so much more creative at home, with the freedom to garden or take walks with the kids between writing assignments. We love visiting the nature center near us, and afterward I feel so refreshed from walking and laughing with the kids as they learn new things that I always end up writing something good! I can't imagine spending eight hours at a 'workstation' now, staring at pictures of my kids, wishing I could be home with them. Regardless of the direction my business takes me, I want to keep working from home."

Are you a WAHM?

Does this sound like you? Do you have the entrepreneurial spirit, resilience, dedication, creativity, independence, realistic attitude, and desire to be a work-at-home mom? If you're not sure, make a gradual transition into working at home. If you think this is what you want to do, but you're scared or unsure, start slowly. You don't have to approach your home business like a bungee jump into the unknown. Begin part-time; work at home while you keep your traditional job. You may even find that being a part-time WAHM works best for you. As I said, WAHMs are all different. You will find the mix that suits you.

IT WAS THE CHICKEN

Even back in high school, I catered to my inner mother, as my instincts leaned more toward feeding my basketball team than scoring points. One evening, before our bus left, I stopped at a restaurant to pick up a "bucket" of chicken from two friends who worked at a well-known fried-chicken restaurant. Every night they had to pick chicken—peel the meat off the bones so the leftover chicken could be used for the next day's sandwiches. They wanted as few pieces left over as possible because they hated picking the chicken. In short, the bucket must have weighed fifteen pounds.

I wasn't a starter on the basketball team, but I was allowed to sit in the back of the bus with the cool girls, the starters. I had the chicken. We had a one-hour bus ride to the game. A glorious, chicken-filled bus ride. We sat all alone in the back of that bus and we ate it all.

We arrived at our competition's school, dressed for the game, and the starters took the floor. They moved across the court with the speed and agility only possible when one has a belly full of greasy fried chicken. After about the first five minutes of the game, we had scored zero points. It became painfully obvious that the chicken feast before the game had been a big mistake.

"What is wrong with you?" our coach screamed at us in the locker room at halftime. She yelled things that have never even been heard in a men's locker room. She grabbed our best guard and screamed at her. "DO YOU HAVE YOUR PERIOD?"

"No, no, it's the chicken," I wanted to confess. But I wasn't brave enough. The rest of the benchwarmers were as baffled as our coach.

The coach never substituted the starters; she made them play that whole, long game. I wanted to tell her, "Take them out of the game. They're chicken-impaired." But I knew the next question would be, "Chicken? Where did they get chicken?"

Maybe she knew the truth after all, and this was her revenge. We ended the game scoring a whopping total of seven points. I believe the game still stands as a record for the lowest score ever for the John Marshall Rockets.

The point is that my team was completely unprepared to play that basketball game, with our bellies full of chicken, and we paid the price.

Now ask yourself if you are prepared to work at home. So you need more education or training before you begin your business? Your local community college may have classes that will help you prepare to meet the challenges you will face as you start to run your home business. Your local library and bookstores are filled with books that will help you get started.

Read, study, and learn everything you can about running your business and you will hit the court ready to play.

YOU MIGHT BE A WAHM

If you call four hours of uninterrupted sleep a good night's rest . . . you might be a WAHM.

If you synchronize your working hours with the *Blue's Clues* TV schedule.

If your refrigerator is the corporate cafeteria.

If you type e-mail while nursing.

If your husband thinks a home-cooked meal is reheated Taco Bell.

If your idea of a great anniversary gift is a new laser printer.

If your work wardrobe consists of jeans, T-shirts, and slippers.

If you wish days were thirty-six hours long.

If you mark the change of seasons by whether or not the UPS man is wearing shorts.

If you spend your free time wondering what it would be like to have free time.

If you consider the playland at McDonald's an off-site meeting facility.

If your children tell their friends, "No, my mom doesn't work, she takes care of us" . . . you might be a WAHM.

PUT AWAY THE BUNNY SLIPPERS

The reality of working at home is often different from the TV commercials we see. You know the ones: Mom is attending a virtual board meeting in her bunny slippers while her toddler plays contentedly in the background.

Here are some of the realistic pros and cons of working at home.

Pros	Cons
You can work in comfortable clothes.	You may end up wearing frumpy sweat suits all the time.
You are free to set your own hours; therefore, you will have more freedom to attend field trips and school plays.	If you don't schedule your time carefully, your business may take over all your free time.
You are the primary caretaker for your children.	You might find it difficult to fit work in with all your other duties.
You'll get a self-esteem boost from running your own business.	Others might not take you seriously because you don't have a "real job."
There will be no holes in your résumé, if and when you decide to return to the traditional workplace.	You have to pay for your own training and education.

Pros	Cons
You are paid directly for the work you do.	You may not get a steady paycheck.
You set an example for your children. They learn about business and the entrepreneurial lifestyle.	Your children may see the bad side of business too—the stress and the headaches. When you work at home, you you can't use your commute time to decompress.
You learn about and stay up-to-date on business regulations and tax laws that relate to home businesses.	The paperwork can be overwhelming.
You are your own boss.	You can't call in sick.

Before you embark on a home business, ask yourself these questions:

How much time do I have to devote to my business?
How much money will I need to start this business?
How will I fit this business into my schedule?
Will I need to buy a computer?
What other office supplies will I need?
How will I get start-up money for the business: savings, loans?
Will I have free time to make sales calls or attend meetings
   without my children?
Am I comfortable marketing and promoting myself?

How can I transfer my skills to this business?

Can I handle the stress and deadlines and do it all well?

Am I able to let my housework slide if I need to in order to complete my work?

You know that you *want* to work at home, you know you *can* work at home. Now . . . *what* to do?

My Parachute Is in the Laundry

Choosing Your Business

When I first started looking for a home business, I was using the Internet mostly to research diabetes information for my daughter Nicki. Then I realized what a great tool the Internet could be for a home business, so I chose Web site design as my first business. With my computer background, it was a logical choice. I concentrated on Web sites for small businesses, and I bartered in exchange for the first few Web sites I created. My first paying job was designing the Web site for my city. I also got a few contracts with larger local businesses, which really helped pay the bills.

During this transition to work-at-home mom, I also read a lot of books. I thought that this might be a good time to find my true calling. I took several personality inventory tests (I'm an INFP) and found out what color my parachute is (blue). Most of the tests suggested that I become either a missionary or a writer. The family wasn't too keen on traveling out of state, much less out of the country, so I turned to writing.

Since working at home was turning out to be such a good solution for my family and me, I started writing about my experiences. I wrote about leaving the traditional workplace to stay at home and the transition from being a working mom to a stay-at-home mom and finally to a work-at-home mom. I have always been a closet writer, but I had never shared my writing with anyone else.

The Internet gave me the anonymity I needed to overcome my shyness, and I posted my writing online. I soon started hearing from other moms all over the world. They were all in the same boat. These were intelligent, well-educated women who really wanted to stay home with their children, yet they wanted (and needed) to work and make money too. Thus my Web site, WAHM.com—The Online Magazine for Work-at-Home Moms, was born.

It started slowly at first, but then word got out, and as more people found the site, it wasn't long before maintaining WAHM.com took over all my time. It quickly grew into a community of moms who wanted to learn from one another, to help one another, to find a home business, and to promote their existing businesses. Those of us who are happily working at home are willing to help out new moms. It's kind of like the coffee klatches of the old days. Instead of gathering around one mom's kitchen table, we're gathering online.

The site was starting to generate income through advertising and affiliate programs, and I really loved working on it. So I decided to stop my Web site design business and concentrate all my work-at-home time on WAHM.com.

FIND YOUR RENO

Now that you've decided that working at home is for you, you just have to figure out what to do. There are several factors to consider, including your skills, how much time you will have to devote to your business, and how much money you will need to make. Think about what you really love to do. How do you spend your free time? Maybe there's a way to turn your passion into a home business.

When we first moved to California, we were determined to show Nicki the sights. We traveled all over the state; we wanted to give her an appreciation for all the natural beauty that was right in our backyard. She was only six, so I guess I shouldn't have expected much, but she was not impressed. "Look! Look!" I'd say as we drove past waterfalls and snow-covered mountains.

"Huh?" She'd look up from her video game for a minute. "Oh, yeah, pretty," she'd say, and then go back to her game.

Until one night when we came up over a hill at the Nevada border, and there in all its neon, electric glory beamed the city of Reno, Nevada.

Nicki was silent for a minute, and then she said, "Now *that* is the most beautiful thing I've seen in my entire life!"

It's that way with home businesses too. Everyone has different tastes and needs, and a business that's perfect for one person might be all wrong for you. If you do what you love, and you are truly devoted to making your business a success, and you are good at what you do, you will have a much better chance of success. If you choose a business simply because someone has told you it will make money, but your heart isn't in it, success is not likely. You have to find the right fit for you, the business that really captures your imagination, your own personal Reno, if you will.

The good news is, your Reno can be just about anything you choose. You can do almost anything from home. There are so many choices, the real challenge is narrowing down all the opportunities and choosing the one that is right for you. It's almost easier to name the jobs that can't be done from home. Okay, so you can't be a bus driver, but I think you might be surprised by the number of businesses that can be run from home.

The Internet is the single greatest factor that is allowing more moms to be able to work at home today. Now, through e-mail and Web sites, we can communicate with people all over the world, at any time of the day or night. We can display our products online, contact clients through e-mail, conduct meetings in chat rooms, and even find jobs online. The best thing about using e-mail for business is that, unlike a phone call, no one knows that Barney is singing his love for me in the background while I'm e-mailing a customer.

If you would like to continue working with your current employer, perhaps on a freelance basis, see if there is a way you can do your work from home, at least part-time. Is it possible to do your work remotely from your home office?

When my oldest daughter was born, my employer had a policy against allowing anyone to work at home. But after I left that job, the company was able to hire me back as a contract employee, and how I got the work done was up to me. So I was able to do a lot of work from home, and I could be much more flexible with my schedule.

As I said, the good news is that you can do just about anything from home . . . and the bad news is, you can do just about anything from home. Sometimes there are just too many choices.

As my youngest daughter's fifth birthday approached, we were trying to decide what to do for her birthday party. There were so many decisions to be made. It was a big birthday for a little girl, so I told her that she could choose where to have her party. I presented her options: Chuck E. Cheese's, McDonald's, the Gym, a pool party, a pizza party. She finally decided on a zoo party. Our local zoo has a great birthday program. A zookeeper brings a few animals to your home, talks about them, and gives the children a chance to pet or hold the animal. The zookeeper might bring a ferret, a snake, or an owl. So, great, she decided on the zoo party. I waited a couple of days just to be sure she wouldn't change her mind. Then, as I was about to send the deposit to the zoo, I asked one last time, "Now, you're sure you want the zoo party?"

"Yes," she said, "I think my friends will like it, and we've never had giraffes at our house before."

Back to the drawing board.

I often get letters from women who really want to work from home, but they don't know what to do. I think to myself, "How can that be? There are so many things to choose from." But perhaps that's part of the problem; just like my daughter, we have too many choices.

So how does one decide what to do, how do you pick your party? I always tell people to think about the things that they like to do, their skills and interests, and try to build a business around that. And look at the businesses other women are running; borrow ideas from them. If you choose something you enjoy, you will have a better chance of success. Again, be careful that you have realistic expectations; we're *work*-at-home moms for a good reason. If someone is trying to sell you on a business, they are going to present their most favorable story and tell you why their company is best.

It is up to you to ask the questions, to find out exactly what is expected and what kind of results the typical person can expect. Find out specifically what animals they will bring to the party, and then make your decision.

My daughter still had her zoo birthday because animals were her "thing" at the time, and she had a great time. I just needed to make sure that she had realistic expectations.

THE ICE-CREAM MAN THEORY OF RELATIVITY

My daughter proved the theory of relativity the other day. No, she's not a child genius, she just loves ice cream.

Ice cream, relativity? Don't see the connection? It's actually quite simple. Normally it takes my daughter thirty-seven minutes from the time I say "Time to go" until she puts on her shoes and gets out to the car.

"Hurry up, hurry up, hurry up," I repeat for thirty-seven minutes.

"I can't goooo any faster!" she will whine.

But when the ice-cream man drives by, she puts on her shoes and goes out the door as if she'd been shot from a cannon. It's as if she has dog hearing for the ice-cream truck's music. We will be sitting quietly in the house . . . I don't hear anything . . . when suddenly she will burst out the door, screaming, "Ice-cream man! Stop! Ice-cream man!" Of course we have ice cream in the freezer, but that's not the same. No, there's something about getting an overpriced ice-cream bar from a smelly old truck that just makes it so *mm-mm* good.

You see, it's all relative. I call it the ice-cream man theory of relativity. How quickly she moves is relative to how close the ice-cream man is to our house. Under normal circumstances, it's not that she *can't* go any faster, she just doesn't *want* to go any faster.

Which makes me think about how often I hear women say "I just can't do that" when they're trying to get started working from home. "I can't sell" or "I can't take the time to do that." When what they really mean is, "I don't want to do that." Think about it, when you *really* want to do something, you find a way to make it happen, don't you? What is your ice-cream truck? What really motivates you and gets you going? What makes you say, "I *can* do that"?

Find your ice-cream truck and then chase after it with everything you've got. You know you *can* do it, you just have to *want* to do it!

SOME QUESTIONS TO ASK YOURSELF AS YOU'RE
CHOOSING YOUR BUSINESS.

What do you love to do?

What are your interests?
How do you spend your free time?
Is this a business you can discuss with excitement with the peo-
ple you meet?

Believe me, your home business can become part of each waking
moment—and even your sleep. I have a friend who decided it was
time to dump her home business when she started having nightmares
of being buried alive in her products. She has since chosen another
business, selling products she loves. So far she's been sleeping peace-
fully; her only business-related dreams are of the tropical islands that
she will visit because she earns such a high home-business income.

Consider your personality. If you're an artistic introvert, a sales
position may not be the best choice. And if you love to be out talking to people all day, computer programming probably wouldn't do.

How much time are you willing to devote to your business?

Are you looking for a part-time business that may make a little
extra money?
Or are you looking for a full-time business that will be your
ticket to fame and fortune?

Look at your schedule first. Consider the amount of time you will
realistically be able to work, and then decide how much and what
kind of work you will be able to do. You don't want to start a busi-

ness, sign contracts with eight clients, and then realize that you can't possibly get it all done.

Some home businesses require that you spend a few hours away from home each day. These are probably best suited for moms with older children so away-from-home time can be scheduled during school hours. If you can be more flexible, you can schedule your away-from-home time for nights and weekends when your husband is home or another family member is available to help.

I tend to bite off more than I can chew. It's a bad habit of mine, so I speak from experience. I find that I'm always saying, "Sure, I'll do that." And then when I sit down and look at my schedule, I wonder what I've gotten myself into. I've gotten a lot better at saying no, but it's hard. I want to teach Sunday school for both daughters, play my violin at church, work in the classroom at school, be on the PTA committee, and run a home business. I've learned that I can try to do everything and do a mediocre job, or do only a few things and do my best. I know moms who spend all their free time attending PTA meetings, leading troops—and all the while ignoring their own children. If you find yourself saying yes too often, ask yourself who you are trying to please. Who are you trying to impress? Will the lady down the street really remember that you baked customized cheesecakes for the spring auction, and more important, do your children really care?

Patti Palilla has been a consultant with Creative Memories for more than ten years. It has taken some adjustment, but now she is able to fit her business into her schedule. She was accustomed to being on the PTA board and the board at her daughter's preschool, chairing committees, and volunteering her time. She found that it is much more healthy for her, and for her family, to just say no sometimes. She realized that she could still stay involved at her daughters' school and still participate in their activities. She says that she has learned to be comfortable being a "worker," and she realizes that she doesn't always have to be a leader or chair every committee.

Have you decided to work from home so you can be there for your children? Then you may need to be flexible with your time, and you may not want to choose a business that will require your attention at any and all hours, night and day. How many hours a day will you be able to work? Will you work only while your children are sleeping, or just during school hours? I choose to work on my Web site and do my writing mostly in the early-morning hours before everyone gets up, and again after the kids are in bed. This works for me but may not be the best solution for you. It may be a good idea to start slowly, and gradually devote more time to your business as you and your family adjust, especially if you have very small children. If you start out trying to work ten hours a day, you're likely to burn out before you even get your business off the ground.

On the other hand, if you decide you want to work only a few hours each week, you can't realistically expect that your business will make you a millionaire. While there are always stories of someone who "makes it big" with minimum time and effort, the reality is that most successful people have put in years of long hours and hard work.

Do you have experience in this business?

Most people find success in a business where they have experience. You don't necessarily have to bring your current job home, but you may be able to find a way to adapt your current occupation to your home business. For some careers, writing for example, it's easy to see how you can transfer your skills to a home business. For others, however, you may have to be a little more creative. Here are some ideas for careers whose home-business applications may not be as obvious.

If your current job is:	*Some jobs you can do at home:*
Accountant	Tax preparation
	Small-business accounting and bookkeeping services
Administrative assistant	Secretarial support for small businesses
	Desktop publishing services
	Typing/word processing services
	Résumé preparation for college students
Attorney	Business consulting and incorporation
	Freelance writing on legal issues
	Trademark registration
	Wills and trusts
Engineer	Contract engineering work
	Software support for small businesses
	Freelance programming
	Computer training
	Web site design
Librarian	Information retrieval
	Internet information searches
	Book-review columnist or Web site publisher

If your current job is:	Some jobs you can do at home:
Marketing	Public relations
	Copywriting
	Marketing-plan preparation
	Event planning
Nurse	Personalized weight-loss consulting
	Teaching childbirth classes
	Lactation consultant
	Chart review for insurance companies
	Home health care
	Nutritional supplements or vitamin sales
Office manager	Professional organizer
	Bookkeeping
	Virtual office manager
Retail saleswoman	Direct sales
Teacher	Tutor
	Provide classes for homeschool students; evaluate students' writing
	Write curricula for homeschool students
	Teach standardized-test preparation classes

If converting your current job is not possible and you've found a business that suits you, talk to as many people as you can to get a feeling for what running your business will really be like. Use *their* experience to educate yourself. You will find most people will be happy to discuss their business with you. If you need to refresh your skills, check out your local college or community college for classes.

A mom I know with a background in early childhood education chose to become a sales representative selling educational products for young children. Because of her education and because she has three boys under age five, the business fits her lifestyle and background perfectly. She has been able to use her knowledge of early childhood development in her presentations. Her workshops for child-care professionals show them the benefits of using the products in their curricula.

Can you realistically make money in this business?

I know a lot of women who have invested hours of their time and energy making craft items or sewing only to realize that they would have to charge a prohibitively high price for their creations to make up for the time they have devoted. Do the math, and ask questions. Just because you've heard of someone making ten thousand dollars a month in a particular business, that doesn't guarantee that you will see the same results.

Jenny Wanderscheid started her Web site, ChildFun.com, more as a hobby than a business. She was doing home child care when she first discovered the Internet and participated on some e-mail discussion lists with other child-care providers. She got some free space with her Internet account on which she could post her own Web site, so she started out small and taught herself how to program her site. When she couldn't figure out how to do something, she would write to other Web site owners whose sites she admired and ask them for help. "Everyone was so nice," she says, "it was great. I was able to learn all the HTML [the programming language of the Web] I needed to run my site." She still wasn't treating her new site as a business, how-ever. She viewed it as a place to post tips and projects for child-care providers—more a hobby, really.

Her light-bulb moment happened accidentally. A few weeks before Christmastime, she noticed that some sites had pictures of Tickle-Me-Elmo and a link to a toy site where the dolls could be purchased. She wrote to the company and asked if she could link to the Elmo doll too. She set up the links and didn't give it another thought, until several weeks later when she received a check for five hundred dollars from the online toy company. She was expecting a fifty-dollar refund check from them, so thinking they had made a mistake, she phoned the com-pany. After a couple of hours, having talked with several customer service personnel, she was told, "No, it's not a mistake. That's not your refund check, that's your commission, from the Tickle-Me-Elmo dolls that sold from your site." She was dumbfounded. That's when she real-ized that there was a way to make money with her site.

Find out how long it will take to start earning income. How much money will you have to invest? How much of your time can you devote to your business? Will you have to pay for occasional child care when you have to meet with clients? It may be possible; but again, do the math.

Can you run this business from *your* home?

Are there zoning restrictions in your community that would prohib-it you from running your business? Some areas place limits on the number of customers or clients that may visit your home each day. There may be restrictions on advertising and manufacturing in your neighborhood.

You will want to check with your community's county or city office and see if there are restrictions regarding the type of business you are considering before you get too far into the process of choosing. It would be a shame to become enthusiastic about a new business idea only to find out that you won't be able to run the business from your home.

You must also consider whether your family will be supportive of your new business endeavor. Will your business take over the garage or a spare bedroom? Butterfly ranching may sound good on paper, but will your children be willing to give up their playroom to make room for the butterflies?

Will your business take over your whole house? I know of a mom whose publishing business grew and grew to a point where her supplies were occupying every bit of free space. She finally made the decision to move her business to outside office space for the sake of her sanity and her marriage. Patti Palilla—the Creative Memories consultant—used to do several workshops in her home each month, and her supplies started to take over her living space. She says she felt as if she were living in a store rather than a house. She has now cut back and keeps her workshops to one or two weekends a month, a balance that works for her business and her family. Discuss these issues with your family and make sure you all agree and are committed to the business.

What if I make a mistake?

If your business isn't working for you, or if you're not happy with your choice, it's okay to try something else. *Don't be afraid to change your mind.*

My husband dresses up as Santa each year at Christmastime and we all go out doing what he calls spreading Christmas cheer. At one stop he went to a home and I waited in the car around the corner. Santa arriving in a Camry would kind of spoil the whole illusion. As he walked back toward the sidewalk, another Camry, exactly like ours, drove by. Surprised to see Santa, the driver slowed down as the car passed him. His fluffy wig and fake glasses obscured his vision, so he assumed it was me and started running after the car. The driver stopped; after all, how often do you have Santa chasing you? As Santa approached the car and reached for the door handle, the occupants came to their senses and realized that a strange man dressed in a cheap Santa suit was trying to get into their car. So they sped up again. Santa hollered out, "Ha-ha, very funny!" and they slowed down again. "Santa's trying to tell us something," I imagined them saying.

So I watched from around the corner, this stop-and-go dance of theirs, all the way down the block. Santa would almost get there and they'd speed up again. He'd holler something and they'd slow down again.

Finally I brought our car around and Mike realized that he was chasing the wrong car. They escaped and probably had a great story to tell when they got home. "We were just driving around, looking at Christmas lights, when this psycho Santa started chasing us." I had a great laugh, and I think Santa even saw the humor in it after he caught his breath.

Many successful businesspeople didn't find success with the first business they started. That's okay. Maybe they were just chasing the wrong car. My friend who sells educational products tried two other home businesses—selling cosmetics and candles—but because she was never passionate about the products, she wasn't very good at sharing the business with others.

Now she doesn't think she could ever go back to the traditional workplace. She says, "I have been home for five years and love the freedom to make my own decisions, grow my business how I choose, and arrange my day my way. I love my home and feel most comfortable here."

Consider these issues while searching for your Reno—your perfect home business. Hopefully, you too will soon be saying, "I love my home and my home business!"

SCAMS

We've all seen the ads that claim to be hiring home workers. Beware: many of them are scams.

The first time we took Dani to Disneyland, she was a little nervous. She watched her big sister go on all the scary rides, but she didn't want any part of them herself. It took some fast talking on my part just to get her to go on the Small World ride. I guess she just didn't know what to expect once that boat went around the corner.

We sat down and she turned to me: "Are we going to go upside down?"

"Upside down? On It's a Small World? Of course not," I tried to reassure her.

She wasn't satisfied. So I pointed out the lack of seat belts on the ride and assured her that Mr. Disney would never, ever send us upside down without a seat belt. After that she was fine. "No seat belts, no worries" became our theme for the rest of the trip.

It's too bad that we don't have such obvious signals in real life. Something that tells us, "Strap on your seat belt, this ride is about to go upside down."

They might not be as obvious, but there are some signs to watch for to protect yourself. Here are some warning signals that will help you weed out the scams from the legitimate jobs.

Businesses that ask for money

They may claim that you need to send money to "show you are serious" or "to cover our costs." This is a giant red flag! Don't do it! You should never have to pay someone to work for them. However getting hired to do a job is different from starting a home business. You will probably have to pay for a starter kit when you begin many direct-sales businesses, but it should be very clear exactly what is in your kit: what you're getting for your money.

Ads that emphasize *work at home*

The ads say they're looking for home workers but are vague about the actual work you will be doing. This is another danger area. They may say that you will be selling "reports" or typing "orders," but again, they are vague regarding the actual products or services.

Ads for assemblers

You will have to pay to get your supplies (first red flag), but here's the big catch. In assembly scams, the company has to approve the work you do. Your first or second batches might be approved, but after you purchase a large quantity of supplies, your work will be rejected because it's "full of flaws," and you will be stuck with your expensive supplies. I have talked to some women who have done legitimate assembly work. They did their work for a local business and weren't asked to pay for supplies up front. Legitimate employers *give* you the materials you need to do your job.

Ads for envelope stuffers

Just don't do it. Think about it. Why would anyone pay two to three dollars to someone simply to put paper in an envelope and apply a stamp? They won't. Most often, after you pay for your supplies, you will be instructed to place ads recruiting others to stuff envelopes.

The envelopes you will be stuffing will be the letters you send out trying to sell others on the same scam you just fell for.

Ads that claim: "No experience necessary" and "Make easy $$$$"

Of course there are jobs that offer on-the-job training, but the majority of employers prefer someone with skills and experience. If the ads lead with these come-ons, watch out. It's another warning signal.

Some businesses aren't outright scams, but many of them are borderline, in my opinion. There are businesses that overemphasize recruiting others on whose sales you will also earn a commission. Recruiters for these businesses get really good at deflecting your arguments; they may make you feel that you'll never be successful if you don't jump at their opportunity. They have many tactics—the best thing you can do is educate yourself, and don't make any quick decisions.

If someone tells you a decision is needed today, walk away. No legitimate business would force you into something you're not ready for. When Patti Palilla thought about becoming a Creative Memories consultant, she held on to her paperwork for three months before she signed up. Now that she's been with the company for more than ten years, she's glad she made the decision. But she just needed time to really think about it and discuss the decision with her family. Good companies realize that each person has her own timetable. If their goal is to help you become successful in the business, they'll allow you the time you need to make your decision. If their goal is just to sign you up, they'll pressure you to make a decision today.

THE PLATE IS HOT

When you're at a restaurant and the server tells you the plate is hot, I'll bet you go ahead and touch the plate anyway. Most people do. Watch, the next time you're out. We get the warning, touch the plate, and then say, "Ouch, that *is* hot!" Same thing if someone says, "This tastes awful!" We pass the offending food around the table and then we say, "*Ewww,* that does taste awful!" It seems to be human nature; we have to find out for ourselves.

I see the same phenomenon all the time among people looking for a home business. We've been warned and warned about scams. We know what to watch out for. But we either ignore the warnings or go ahead and fall for the same scams all over again. Why do we have to find out for ourselves? Do we think we're smarter than everyone else is?

Or is it just wishful thinking? The claims sound so good; we really want them to be true. We want to believe that this time, someone will pay us three dollars to lick an envelope and Bill Gates really will send us ten thousand dollars for forwarding e-mail. It would be so easy, if only it were true. The women I know who are successful in their home businesses have all achieved their success through a lot of hard work.

Next time you're considering sending money to someone who is making outrageous claims, stop and think. This time won't be different; once a scam, always a scam. Use common sense, and if it sounds too good to be true, it *is* too good to be true.

Before you get burned, just remember, the plate is hot.

SURVIVAL TIPS FROM SISTER ZOOS
How Did You Choose Your Business?

I was a mortgage broker when I was introduced to the concept of dipping strawberries into chocolate. I needed a gimmick to market myself to real estate agents and I quickly turned a fun hobby into a signature gift as a mortgage agent. I wrapped up dipped berries in gift baskets and presented them at each and every annual holiday from Easter to St. Patrick's Day! I was always amazed at how the agents went crazy over the berries.

Shari F., California, Berries.com

I chose medical transcription because I was already very familiar with the medical field. I am a speech-language pathologist. I felt that I had a very strong background in medical terminology and wanted to stay in the medical field. After my son was born, I knew right away that I was not going back to work outside the home. I loved being a mother, and I could not even conceive of leaving him in day care. Still, we needed more than one income. I love doing medical transcription because, believe it or not, I love to type. And I love medical terminology. That may sound weird to some people, but I feel it is my gift. I've finally found my niche in life.

Julie T., Alabama

I chose a business in the field I had the most experience in, travel and vacation rentals. I took some time to get started; I pounded on doors and did thousands of hand-addressed mailings. My family joins me when I travel to places to work out exchanges. I added more services as I could handle them. I knew I wanted to be a full-service property management and vacation rental business, so I started with a housecleaning department, then I added full-scale property management, then small home repairs. It took several months between each step, but it was worth it. Patience, patience.

Cher B., Vermont, bpmofstowe.com

A lifestyle change prompted me to make the transition from my corporate job in international advertising to a home business. My husband accepted a job that moved us from Georgia to California. At that time we decided that I would stay home full-time with our children. A friend of mine had attended a Creative Memories workshop and she told me about the opportunity. I loved the products and the mission of the business. I was personally overwhelmed by our accumulation of photos, so I knew that this was a service that I could use myself and that I'd feel good about bringing to others.

Patti P., California

I really wasn't looking to work at home. . . . It found me.

I had learned a lot about advertising and marketing, courtesy of my employers over the years, and had started a mobile mechanics business with my husband. I was writing marketing plans and designing all the advertising for both businesses. Customers started phoning to ask who did our artwork and brochures.

What started off as a favor has turned into a full-time business.

Laura T., California

I started my home business by accident. Once I realized that no one was going to visit my little homepage full of links, I knew I had to start adding content and networking. That was when I first published articles on my site.

Amanda F., Wisconsin, FamilyCorner.com

I really liked the first business I chose. I think that it was a good opportunity, but the people who got me started focused on recruiting and not the products, and I didn't want to do that. That's why I decided to leave. I work from home for a business-consulting organization in my area, and I also started selling Towel Buddies because I love them. I also like the fact that they are made by stay-at-home moms, and the company focuses on the products and not recruiting.

Molly R., West Virginia

PROBLEM
I can't decide which home business is right for me.

SOLUTIONS FROM SISTER ZOOS
If the business is *really* right for you, you almost shouldn't need to ask this question. The best business for you will, if you really get to understand the subject, be a no-brainer. You won't be able to say no, let alone wonder which one to say yes to.

Nancy P., California

You have to be very careful, because indecision makes you susceptible to scams. Know what you love to do, and find a need that you can fill. Listen to your friends and neighbors talk about what they wish they could hire someone to do. Brainstorm from there. But do not pay anyone a dime for a business scheme if the money you could make is more exciting to you than the job you would do to earn it.

Jamie R., Florida

Go with what you're good at! Figure out what you really enjoy doing, and choose a business that complements you. Example: If you love to cook, go with Tupperware or Pampered Chef, start a catering business, or start your own recipe and cooking tips Web site. Do what you love, and you'll love what you do.

Lynn T., Tennessee

Why choose just one? Many moms have two or three businesses that they run from home. Start with one, and evolve as time passes. You may not grow to love every business, but you never know.

Calissa L., Florida

The most helpful hint I can think of is that you can't choose a business because you think it will earn a huge profit in a short amount of time. The majority of us work-at-home moms have put work, time, and a lot of effort into our businesses; that's how we make money. Love what you do, it is worth it.

Joyce E., Georgia

You need to do something that you *love*. Choosing the right business should not be a difficult decision. With all the distractions you're going to face as a WAHM, you need to be sure that you'll want to go and work; think about what makes you happy and choose something that will give you joy.

Andrea K., Ontario

Chart it out. Make a column with items such as:

Start-up costs

Training time needed

Accessibility of customers

Current competition

Obsolescence (Will this business always be needed?)

Any other variable factor

Across the top, list your various ideas.

Now, make notes in each area and boil it all down to which one works the best for you. Most important, make sure your listed businesses all stem from something that you enjoy; otherwise, it'll be no more fun than an office job!

Mia C., Wisconsin

Make lists of likes and dislikes, but make sure you know your dislikes. Many people don't realize how many of their dislikes they will have to do when they are in business for themselves.

Val S., Washington

YOUR BUSINESS PLAN

Many WAHMs are tempted to skip this step, but it will really help you clarify your strategy and goals. Unless you're seeking financing, your business plan doesn't have to be long and formal. Consider these areas as you prepare your plan.

- What is your business?
  What products will you sell or what service will you provide? In this section, describe in detail your product or service and your vision for your business.

  _____

  _____

  _____

- Who will buy this product or service?
  Think about your potential customers. Why do people need what you have to offer? How and when will you be able to sell your service or product? Will you meet your customers face-to-face? Will you sell your products online?

  _____

  _____

  _____

- Who is your competition?
  Look at other businesses. Is there anyone else providing your product or service? What will you do differently? Why will people buy from you instead of your competitors? Will you be

able to use your status as a work-at-home mom to your advantage to market to other moms or people who support your lifestyle?

_____

_____

_____

- What will your costs be?
  Examine all your expenses, start-up costs, marketing costs, and ongoing costs. How much will you charge? Is there real profit potential?

_____

_____

_____

- How will people find out about your business?
  How will you promote the business and find new customers? Keep the four Ps in mind: Product, Placement, Promotion, and Price. What product are you selling? From where will you sell it? Mail order, direct sales, boutiques? How much will you spend promoting it? At what price will you sell it?

_____

_____

_____

- How will you manage your home and business?
  Think about how you will integrate your business into your family's schedule. How will you handle sick days? Will you travel for business? Do you have a support system established that can help you when you have deadlines or sick children? Will your business be flexible enough that you can work around your family's schedule?

_____

_____

_____

Hopefully, this has gotten you started organizing your thoughts and thinking like a manager. Whether you're starting small or dreaming big, you need to have a plan. Come back to this plan again as your business grows—review what you've written and update and revise it as needed. This will be your guide as you make future business decisions.

Okay, you're ready to go. You've chosen your business, and now you're ready to flip the switch. Well . . . the transition may not be _quite_ that easy.

5

Wild Animals in Captivity

Making the Transition

I'm a Housewife?

I've talked to so many women who have a particularly difficult time with this. The first time someone called me a housewife, I had an identity crisis.

My insurance agent was asking: Name? Address? Occupation? Occupation . . . I wasn't sure how to answer that one, being new to the stay-at-home business. "I . . . I'm . . . I guess I'm a mom," I answered. I watched him write in the occupation line: "Housewife." I couldn't believe it! How could I, one who has never considered the relative merits of different brands of fabric softener, be labeled a housewife? June Cleaver was a housewife, but me? I didn't think so.

I complained to my husband that night, "All my life, I've been something. A student, an engineer, but what am I now?"

I didn't realize my daughter had been listening, she piped in with her answer, "You're a MOM!" she said, just as I answered, "What am I now? Nothing!"

She was so proud to have figured out the answer and the look on her face when she heard me say "nothing" broke my heart. She was right; I'm a mom above all else. I've never felt like a nothing since that moment.

As you make the transition from working mom to work-at-home mom, I think you, too, will find that "mom" is the best job description you've ever had.

But it isn't always a smooth transition. I was accustomed to putting on a suit, pumps, and panty hose, waving good-bye, and driving off to work. All of a sudden I was wearing a T-shirt and jeans, standing over the toilet with my daughter, waving and saying, "Bye-bye poopy. Have a nice ride!" What was happening? I must admit, I was a little envious of my husband and his work in the "adult world."

It's such a drastic change, it can be kind of scary. I think that the average mom, after spending a good amount of time at home alone with her children, is ready—to paraphrase Thoreau—"to fasten herself like a bloodsucker to any full-blooded man or woman who comes her way."

Believe it or not, this transition problem has been around forever. I actually found records of the very first work-at-home mom in the history of humanity. Let's take a peek into Christy Cave-Dweller's diary:

Dear Diary: I killed my first saber-toothed tiger today. I'm proud of the fact that I can hunt along with the men. This new freedom to do what I want to do is sooo liberating.

Dear Diary: Yesterday after dinner, Jimmy from the other village knocked me over the head and dragged me off to his cave. I'm so happy.

Dear Diary: Now that Jimmy Junior is on the way, we've decided that I will continue to hunt as I did before Jim dragged me to his cave. Linda, one of the women who stays at her cave all day, will take care of Junior while I'm away. I don't know how she can stand being in that cave all day. I need more mental stimulation than that!

Dear Diary: Things aren't working out exactly as I had planned. When I'm hunting, I miss Junior more than you can imagine. Then when I get home, I still have more work to do. All Big Jim does is complain that the cave is always a mess. Who has time to do everything?

Dear Diary: All the extra food we get from my hunting trips goes to pay Linda for watching Jim Junior. What's the point of being away from home all day if I have nothing to show for it?

Dear Diary: Margo and Lisa, the other "hunting mothers," both say I'm helping Junior by showing him that women can be hunters too. I think all he's learning is that Linda is there to hug him when he's sad and I'm not there.

THE FIRST WAHM

Dear Diary: I decided to quit hunting today. We will get by somehow. Margo called me a cave-wife; I don't really care for that. I'm thinking of doing some kind of work from home. I notice a lot of the food we bring home spoils before we can eat it. If only we had some kind of containers that would keep the food fresh. *Hmmm . . .* I wonder . . .

WHAT'S YOUR TITLE?

I was driving the car and Dani was riding next to me, singing along with the radio. Suddenly Dani interrupted the song. "Mom? Will I always be able to call you Mom?"

"Of course, Dani. What else would you call me?"

"Well, I was just thinking. When I get older, I might have to call you something else."

What do you want people to call you? It does make a big difference—in your attitude and in how others see you. Are you really taking your business seriously? Do you give yourself credit for all the work you do?

I've talked to a lot of work-at-home moms who have told me that they noticed a difference in their businesses as soon as they gave themselves a title. Instead of minimizing their work, they spoke as if they were already successful: "I'm a writer." "I design Web sites." "I'm a painter." "I'm a graphic designer." "I'm a business owner."

One day when Dani was three, I took her out for breakfast. We stopped at a bakery and bought milk, coffee, and a couple of doughnuts. As she ate her breakfast, she said, "Mom, this is the best bagel I've ever had!" I started to correct her, to tell her that these weren't bagels at all, but a new thing called doughnuts . . . but then I decided not to. Maybe I would let her go on for a while longer, thinking that these "good bagels" were a great new discovery. Now, instead of

changing her vocabulary, we all call doughnuts "good bagels."

Labels may not seem important on the surface, but how many times have you described yourself as "just a mom"? Be careful that you don't diminish your role as a mom and as a businesswoman too. We're breaking new ground here. Not many people are aware of the opportunities for working from home or what a great solution it can be for families today.

When people ask, "What do you do?" or "Do you work?" do you find yourself at a loss for words? Prepare an answer to have ready. These questions become great opportunities to enlighten others about the wonderful world of working at home. One mom I know met her business partner as a result of her quick response to such a situation. She was attending her son's baseball game when another mom rushed up to catch the final inning. "You're so lucky you don't have to work," she told my friend. "I can never get to these games on time." Instead of getting angry or defensive, my friend simply replied, "Oh, but I do work. I run a custom furniture business from my home." It turned out the other mom was a marketing specialist wrestling with whether or not to quit her job. Intrigued by my friend's business, she started asking questions. They soon teamed up, combining the artistic talents of one mom with the sales and marketing expertise of the other, to create a successful business.

To an outsider, it may appear that you have loads of free time. After all, you are home all day. How many people know about the frenzy of activity that goes on behind closed doors? So, if you're a WAHM, don't be afraid to claim your title.

A rose by any other name may smell as sweet, and a doughnut doesn't become fat-free just by calling it a bagel. But a work-at-home mom deserves all the credit she can get. So give yourself credit for everything you do by giving yourself a title. Watch it make a difference for you too.

And while I may change careers again someday, I'll always be Mom to my girls.

Don't Assume Everything Will Be Perfect from the Start

Starting a home business is like adding another member to your family. As you can imagine, this will require some adjustment on everyone's part. Your priorities and expectations will determine how well you all adjust; communication, help, and humor will make the transition easier.

Sure there will be bumps. A friend of mine, Sue, was running a Web site and had a small mailing list of members to whom she sent e-mail updates and Web site announcements. She and her husband were going through a particularly tense time in their marriage and had had a bad fight the night before. The next day as she was trying to think of something she could do to make up to her husband, she decided to use her creative writing talents and compose a little story about the two of them. She wrote a steamy, and I mean steamy, story starring the two of them. She sent it to her husband's e-mail address, or so she thought. Imagine her horror when the members of her mailing list started sending her angry e-mails. That's when she realized that she had accidentally sent her very private e-mail to her entire mailing list. They all started writing back to her, complaining about the smut she was sending out. Was she out of her mind? they demanded to know. Thinking quickly, she explained that her site had been hacked and someone had taken control of her e-mail and sent the offensive e-mail without her knowledge. A few of her members bought it, a few gave her a wink and a nudge, and about half unsubscribed from her list.

One of my worst experiences happened a few years ago. When I first started my home business, I signed up for an 800 number. That summer we took a long vacation and the bill got mixed up and didn't get paid.

I hadn't realized that the number was disconnected—I never got that many calls on it anyway—until it was too late. I found out that the number had been reassigned when someone alerted me to the fact that when they called my 800 number, they got a phone sex line.

You can imagine the shock when someone who thinks they're calling for stay-at-home information instead hears a sultry voice say, "Don't just sit there with your hand in your pants. . . ."

I'm almost to the point where I can laugh about it, but not quite.

WHERE'S *MY* PARTY?

Have you ever felt like you just didn't fit in?

My family was invited to two parties recently. The first was attended mostly by working moms. Their conversations centered on nannies and flextime, benefit packages, maternity leave, and vacation days. I tried to act interested in what they were saying, I really did. One mom had recently left her job, but she made it clear that she hadn't done so to stay at home with her children. "We're keeping our nanny!" she said. I just couldn't relate.

Mostly stay-at-home moms attended the next party. It was held in a sparkling home, the party was beautifully organized, and our hostess served plenty of homemade goodies. I found myself wishing I had the time to coordinate such a party.

Of course, both groups of moms, stay-at-home and working moms, face unique challenges.

Stay-at-home moms have to work within a one-income budget.

They have the challenge of keeping their children entertained and creatively occupied. Working moms deal with two full-time jobs, their careers and running their households. Plus all the stress and frustration associated with having to "do it all."

But the party experiences left me feeling unsettled. I felt like I just didn't fit in anywhere. Work-at-home moms are in the middle—we're working, but we're home too. There are things we have to give up when we choose the work-at-home lifestyle, but I think the benefits make up for it. I just wish there were more of us.

I'm looking forward to the day when I can attend a party with other work-at-home moms. There may not be enough of us . . . yet . . . but give us time. As more and more women are discovering the benefits of working at home, I'll bet it won't be long before I'm partying with a room full of work-at-home moms.

STAYING POSITIVE

Oprah Calling

I've had several moments since I started my business when I've thought, "This is it. This is my big break." But it will only be a momentary blip of success, and I go back to work again. Slowly, surely, the business is growing, but I've never reached that big boom I had been hoping for. Now I know better. I have realized that the path to success is slow and steady. Sure you hear about overnight successes every now and then, but if you really dig into their stories, you'll hear about years and years of hard work that led up to the "big break."

There are days when I imagine that the next phone call will be an agent calling with a great book deal, or a big investing group calling to ask where they should send the check, but I have my down days too. Some days I'm sure that this will never work out and that there will never be another visitor to my Web site. I will look back years from now and wonder why I ever devoted so much time and energy to such a losing proposition.

So I decide that I need a break. To cheer myself up, I pack up the car and the kids and we head to the zoo for the day (the real zoo). We eat junk food and stroll around and just waste time in general.

Inevitably, my thoughts creep back to my business again. I fantasize that while I'm gone, Oprah will call, but I won't be home. She will leave a message saying that they're looking for a woman to talk about work-at-home moms on her show, and they would love to have me come to Chicago, but I have to call her back before 5:00 that

day or they will call someone else. And I don't get the message until late that night because I've decided to take the girls to the zoo for the day. There we are, having a great time at the zoo, but I can't stop thinking about Oprah. So I start to get a little panicked, and I call my voice mail, just to check.

But there aren't any messages, and of course there *really* isn't any message from Oprah or her producers, so I hang up and think about what an idiot I am.

I don't think I'm alone in my fantasies, at least I hope not. From the conversations I've had with other work-at-home moms, these ups and downs are pretty common. The fantasies just seem to be a part of being self-employed. If you're someone who is deciding whether a home business is right for you, keep this in mind. You won't have many routine, boring days in front of you. It can be a roller coaster, this home business lifestyle, but I'm willing to stay put for the ride. In fact, I prefer it. So if you think you're up for a few laps on the coaster, buy your ticket and join us. I don't think you'll regret it.

(Memo to Oprah: You can call anytime!)

Believe it or not, just a few weeks after I wrote this, the unbelievable actually happened. . . . Read on.

Oprah Called!

What a week.

It was a Wednesday; the phone rang at about 3:00.

"Cheryl? This is John Doe (name cleverly changed to protect the innocent) from the *Oprah Show*.

I'm not kidding, it really was Oprah's show, calling me! Can you believe it?

We talked about WAHM.com for a while and then he said, "Don't get excited, but would you like to share your story with Oprah, and are you available next Tuesday?"

Don't get excited? That's like saying, "Eat this coconut cream pie but don't gain weight."

Of course I was available. I didn't mention that we were actually planning a trip to Disneyland. "Hey, kids, Chicago can be fun too!" I hung up with the understanding that this was all very up in the air, but a possibility.

After I was off the phone I started jumping around the house and screaming, "That was Oprah! That was Oprah!" My daughter hid behind the couch. I don't think she was exactly sure what an oprah was, but she wasn't sticking around to find out.

We went shopping and I bought an Oprah outfit, which I had already preselected for just this occasion. I calculated how much weight I could lose in five days (thirty pounds), and I got my hair cut. And then I waited, and waited. After a couple of days it became apparent that I wasn't going to be on the show after all. We continued with our Disney vacation plans, taking Chicago clothes with us just in case, and I continued to call home to check messages.

My Oprah contact did call back and said that they had enough people for the show but they liked my story and might be able to work it into a future show. Oh, well, it was exciting while it lasted.

We had a great time at Disneyland, and at least I had a nice haircut and I lost a few pounds.

My husband says that Tony Robbins is my imaginary friend because I'm always so positive. I'd like to tell you that I picked myself up, and brushed myself off, and the next day I made a million dollars and Barbara Walters called! But Tony must have been on vacation this time because as I look back on this experience, the thing I remember most is how disappointed I was.

Visualize Your Success . . . Sometimes

Speaking of imaginary friends, my girls both had four. They still show up from time to time. My oldest started out with just two, Boy and Girl. Then Lisa came along, and finally Johnson. Where did Johnson come from? We had no idea. We knew they had gotten out of hand when we had to return home one day because Nicki had forgotten her "friends" at home. Eventually we had her teach them that they could just run alongside the car if they were left behind and jump in on the fly. Can you imagine having to explain missing a dentist appointment because of them? "Sorry we're late, but we left Johnson at home." I don't think so.

I'm guessing that you probably had a pretty active imagination when you were younger too. Did you have imaginary friends, or did you dream about what your life would be like when you grew up? Why stop dreaming now that you're an adult?

Visualize your success. Picture yourself reaching your goals in really concrete ways. If you have a dream house, cut out a picture and put it on your refrigerator. Imagine yourself at a book signing for your latest best-seller or signing your big contract.

I usually take my own advice and dream about my next success. But sometimes it is difficult to get over disappointments in my business, or to keep going when things aren't going well. I don't have any great insight for you into how to get through those times other than, just give it time. What I really wanted to do after the Oprah Incident, as it has come to be known, was to sleep until noon, then get up and watch *All My Children* while eating a banana split and drinking a margarita, and then go back to bed.

Of course, I couldn't do that, we were out of bananas.

PROBLEM

I miss my corporate identity. I know this is important work, but sometimes I can't help feeling that I'm "just" a mom.

SOLUTIONS FROM SISTER ZOOS

Ugh, I hate those three words! Being a mom is the most important job in the world. And to think that we can do the most important job in the world and run a business and keep everyone in clean underwear, and we get to do it all without having to wear panty hose every single day. Who needs a "corporate identity"?

Jamie R., Florida

A title doesn't mean you're making money. I know doctors who are in debt because they cannot manage money. It's not your title that makes money; it is how well you handle what you earn.

Calissa L., Florida

Being a mom is most likely the most important job that you'll ever have, so don't look down on yourself for that. As for corporate identity, you can still have an important identity within a home business. I paid for and attended a corporate workshop to get my title of Certified Lifestyle Consultant, complete with certificate on the wall. If you treat your home business seriously, there's no reason that you cannot give yourself a title and expect that others will take it seriously as well. Use your title on your business cards and any other correspondence.

Kelly S., Michigan

Once the baby was sleeping through the night, I found that resuming my morning ritual helped a lot. I got up before my husband, took a shower, enjoyed a cup of coffee all to myself—just like I did while working. The only change being that this time I didn't jump in the car to go to the office. Just the smell of the coffee made me feel better—more like my old "corporate self," so that I didn't miss it so much anymore.

Margaret Q., Michigan

There are lots of businesses out there that have recognition programs for their representatives. Try looking for a business that offers awards, rewards, and perks for their top performers. This can help give you back some of the recognition you were used to in the corporate world.

Rachael H., Florida

Unfortunately, our society does that to moms. It's up to you to rebuild that confidence in yourself by doing your best work and remembering to take care of yourself too. When you're able to take time for yourself, even if it's just thirty minutes a day, you'll be a better mom and a better entrepreneur. And don't forget to get out at least once a month with other adults. You might even consider starting a club of work-at-home moms in your community, and do some networking every month.

Mia C., Wisconsin

Go to lunch or dinner regularly with people who still work in the corporate world. It won't take long for you to realize that it's just a case of the grass looking greener on the other side of the fence. You will remember the things you didn't like about working outside the home, and you will appreciate the benefits of working from home all over again.

Alanna W., Oklahoma

I'm in uncharted waters here regarding corporate identity, but I understand the loss of one's identity to marriage and parenthood. You are no longer Mary Jane Doe but Mrs. Somebody, and Someone's mother. Reestablish yourself first, finding what makes you more individual than the role confinements your situation demands.

Rose Marie B., New York

Now just to make sure everything continues to run smoothly, you need to establish some ground rules.

6

Don't Feed the Animals

Rules and Regulations

Rules

Rule No. 1: Determine Your Priorities

Defining what you expect from your business and family is important as you start your business. What are your priorities? Do you need to have a clean house? Make lots of money? Have free time for yourself? Will your spouse be supportive? Will your children be expected to help with the business or will the business be off-limits to them? Will you work regular hours?

For me, one of my top priorities is my family, which is why I chose a home business in the first place. Besides, God willing, I'll have many, many years to work after my children are grown. When all is said and done, I would rather say I've had a marginally successful business and a successful family life than have enjoyed a phenomenally successful business career and only a marginally successful family life. And I do believe that it's possible to combine business and family successfully. When I first started my business, I went back to a list of priorities I had written as a college assignment. I sat down and listed all the things that were important to me. They fell under such categories as family, health, business, religion, money, fun and recreation, security, and recognition.

I then numbered them to determine my priorities. I'm amazed and somewhat embarrassed when I look back on the first list I wrote while I was still in college. Aging and life experiences have changed me quite a bit, thank goodness. I won't share the entire list with you, but I will say that fun and recreation ranked much higher twenty years ago than they do now. Doing this exercise may make you think about things a little differently, and it will help you clarify your priorities.

WAHMs: IN THE NEUTRAL ZONE
OF THE MOMMY WARS

No. 2: Adjust Your Expectations

Notice I didn't say lower your expectations. Having worked in software, I've acquired the ability to turn a bug into a feature. If a computer doesn't work exactly as anticipated, a good software engineer will find a way to turn that into a feature of the program: "The date reads January 1, 1900? Right, we meant to do that. It gives us the feeling of going back to a more relaxed time."

You can look at household tasks in the same way. As Joan Rivers said, "I don't clean my bathtub anymore. When I have company, I just take a marker and label the bathtub ring, 'Fill to Here.'" Now, that's turning what most people would see as a problem into a feature.

If my house were ever burglarized, the crooks would just turn around and leave without taking anything. They would think someone had beaten them to the job. My house is preransacked! That's a feature. You may not be comfortable letting things slide quite that much; however, you'd be well advised to find your own comfort level and relax a little.

Most moms find that the first days running our home businesses are like a honeymoon. We are filled with enthusiasm and excitement. We have planned and prepared and feel like nothing can stand in our way. I'll never forget the feeling I had when I got my first home-business contract. I walked with my head held higher. I felt like putting a sign around my neck: I AM A BUSINESSWOMAN!"

Then reality sets in, and reality doesn't always meet our expectations. The jobs might not come along regularly. The day-to-day challenges of running a business start to take their toll. A lot of moms give up at this stage. Adjust your expectations and realize that this is normal and to be expected. Also keep your priorities clear; go back to your priority list. Remind yourself why you started the business in the first place, and keep your focus on your long-term goals.

Rule No. 3: Enlist Support

My little girl came home from school the other day and demanded, "Kiss me on the lips, Mom."

"But Dani," I said, "I can't kiss you. You know I'm sick. I don't want to make you sick too."

"I know, Mom, that's the point. I want to catch your cold."

It turned out that the next day was mile-run day at her school, and she was looking for any way to get out of it. I managed to keep her healthy through the night, gave her a pep talk the next morning, and sent her off to school.

She was surprisingly upbeat when I picked her up that afternoon. She had finished the run with a good time and agreed that it wasn't so bad after all. In fact, she was pretty proud of herself.

Thinking my pep talk had done the trick, I pressed for more information. "So, as you were running, were you thinking about what I told you this morning?"

"No, Mom. You didn't help me at all. The pacers helped me finish."

"Pacers?"

"The big kids, fifth and sixth graders. They ran beside me when I slowed down, talked to me, and kept me going."

Pacers. What a great idea. Who couldn't use a pacer every day? Not just for exercise encouragement but for encouragement in everything.

Do you have a pacer in your life? Do you have someone who "runs beside you" when you slow down or need a little extra encouragement? Do you have a pacer who keeps you motivated to reach your business goals when you feel like you just can't go on? Is it your spouse, a good friend, a business associate?

If you don't have a pacer in life already, take advantage of local networking groups, support groups, and online support groups. Talk to other moms at home, other moms who are working at home, if you can. You will find many friendly moms who will be happy to give you advice and encouragement. They will understand what you're going through, and often just talking to someone else who understands can help you get through the tough times.

With a pacer, you may find that your goals are a little easier to reach, and you won't be tempted to do anything drastic (like kiss on the lips) to avoid running the race.

Rule No. 4: Communicate

Don't expect your spouse and children to be psychic. If you require something of them, let them know. Now that you've established your priorities and expectations, communicate them to your family. And be specific. I get more help if I say to my husband, "Please empty the dishwasher and make eggs and toast for the girls" than if I just ask, "Will you help in the kitchen?"

I also tell my family the details of my business problems or successes, and I sometimes discuss questions I have with them. We are always talking. We make a point of sitting down for meals together so we can all share what is happening in our lives. We usually keep the radio off in the car and use this time for talking too. We set goals together and choose something fun that we will all do with the business money when our goal is reached. It can be as simple as a night out for ice cream or as big as a family vacation. This way, we all reap the rewards of the business. And I often get great ideas from my husband and my daughters. When we were discussing the marketing plan for my first book, my daughter suggested putting "This is *not* Cheryl's book" on all of the other books at the bookstore. Maybe not the most practical suggestion, but not a bad idea.

Rule No. 5: Accept Help

Since time is a limited resource, you'll want to spend it in the most efficient manner possible. If you're billing work out at the rate of forty dollars an hour and can hire someone to do housecleaning or yard work for ten dollars an hour, do it. (And then send me the person's number.) No one will think less of you if you don't clean your own toilets.

Face the fact that you can't do everything. Get out your priority list again. If you don't want to turn over full-time care of your children to someone else, explore other options. Maybe have a sitter come into your home occasionally or share part-time child care with another home-based parent. Then have your client meetings and do your work during those hours. Hire a neighborhood teenager to help out with chores around the house. Subcontract with other moms to handle some business tasks or pay them a commission for sales help.

Help is out there; accept it.

Rule No. 6: Be Professional, Hire Professionals

Treat your business like a business. Open a separate checking account for your business and keep all financial transactions separate from your personal account. Always present a professional image through your résumé, e-mails, and telephone conversations. When you're working at home, you often don't have the advantage of being able to make a face-to-face impression, so you have to be extra careful to be professional in all your business communication.

Don't expect to understand or know all the laws and regulations about running a business. Find a good accountant and a lawyer. Know your weak points and hire professionals to fill the gaps. If you concentrate on your strengths and let your team of professionals handle the rest, you'll have a much better chance of success.

Rule No. 7: Use Technology to Your Advantage

There are many gadgets that make our work-at-home lives easier. Here are a few that you can use to help you work more efficiently. For me, the two simple but lifesaving tools are my two-line cordless phone and my cable modem. On my two-line phone, the business line has a different ring from our personal line, so it's easy to tell when a business call is coming in. My children know that when the business line rings, they need to be quiet. I don't always choose to answer if we're in the middle of something—I let it go to voice mail. But if I'm expecting a call, they know the drill. As for the cable modem, I couldn't accomplish half of what I do in a day if I had to wait for pages to download through a dial-up!

- *Computer.* This one kind of goes without saying because a computer is almost essential for every work-at-home mom. With a computer you can do your bookkeeping, create marketing materials, design a Web site for your business, use e-mail to communicate with customers from all over the world, and connect online with other work-at-home moms. The best thing about e-mail is that you can do business at any time of the day or night, and no one can hear what's going on in the background while you're typing your e-mail.

- *Cellular phone.* A cellular phone is a great time-saver. You can make calls while you're waiting to pick up your children at school or out at the park. A note of caution, however: driving requires all your attention. No call is so important that it can't wait until you stop the car. So use your cell phone when you're away from home but don't take any safety risks for the sake of a few minutes on the phone.

- *Voice mail.* The advantage of voice mail over a standard answering machine is that callers can leave messages if your line is busy. If you have only one phone line and you're online a lot, use voice mail and your customers will never get a busy signal.

- *Caller ID.* Caller ID helps you determine which calls should be answered right away and which can go to voice mail. Combine caller ID with a cordless phone and you have even more freedom.
- *Personal digital assistant (PDA).* A PDA is a powerful little computer. You can keep track of your schedule, include your address book, check your e-mail, and take notes. Think of it as an organizer that fits in the palm of your hand.
- *Digital voice recorder.* If you find you get your best ideas at the most inopportune moments, a digital voice recorder will come in handy. Many recorders also come with software that can learn your voice patterns. When the recorder is connected to your computer, it converts your speech to text.

Tools don't have to be high-tech to be useful. When I asked work-at-home moms about their favorite work-at-home tools, some of their answers were decidedly low-tech. Among their favorites were pocket-size notebooks, planners, and slow cookers.

Use these gadgets and tools to your advantage and you will simplify your work and home life.

REGULATIONS

You have several choices when contemplating the structure of your business.

Sole Proprietorship

A sole proprietorship is the least expensive and least complicated type of business. You and your business are viewed as the same, and you will be personally liable for any losses your business incurs. Regulations vary from state to state, but if you are doing business in a name other than your own, you will most likely need to register as a DBA (Doing Business As).

Corporation

The main advantage you get when you incorporate is some protection from personal liability. Your corporation is separate from you as an individual. It can also make your business seem more substantial; there is status that comes with the CEO title. You will have your board of directors to advise you and help you grow your business. However, a corporation is more complicated and expensive to establish and maintain than a sole proprietorship or a partnership.

Profit or Nonprofit

If you choose to incorporate as a nonprofit, it doesn't mean that you can't make any money. The corporate directors can still be paid a salary. However, the rules are complicated, and you definitely need legal advice from an attorney familiar with nonprofit incorporation if you are thinking about going the nonprofit route. Religious, charitable, and educational companies are examples of some businesses that may qualify for nonprofit status.

Partnership

If you are working on your business with a friend, you're usually considered partners whether or not you have filed a formal partnership agreement. Working in a partnership gives you someone with whom you can share your business expenses and burdens, and you can combine your resources to build the business. But you will also be personally responsible for your partner's business liabilities, and no matter how well you are getting along now, you may have serious disagreements. Partnerships almost always start happily; formal agreements make for happy endings too.

You may change the structure of your business as your business grows and your needs change. For example, you may wish to start as a sole proprietor and incorporate at a later date. It is essential that you consult with your attorney and accountant to determine which structure is best for you.

TIPS FROM A SISTER ZOO

Debbie Williams, organizing coach and founder of OrganizedTimes.com, offers these tips for office organization and family office rules.

OFFICE ORGANIZATION

Store files in portable crate systems or in a vertical desktop rack. Hang shoe or jewelry organizers over the doors for office supplies, books, and tapes. Bulletin boards placed around the room at eye level provide easy viewing while you are seated at your desk. Keep your office free of clutter by providing a dedicated place for everything. Purchase stackable bins for processing paperwork. Purchase a drawer divider for stationery and desk supplies. Inform family members where to deliver incoming correspondence. Utilize a master calendar or wipe-off board for coordinating special projects. Scan articles and clip and file them in a folder for reading at a later date. Maintain a workable follow-up system with an index-card file or accordion file.

OFFICE TRAFFIC

Monitor traffic in your office without upsetting family members by making light of it. Design a traffic light for your office door and explain the rules to your children. Red light means Stop, do not enter while I'm working. Yellow light means Enter quietly and slowly; green lights means Come on in and visit. Use a kitchen timer in your office so your children can monitor your work time. Explain that when the timer dings you will be finished with your work and ready to spend some quality time with them.

PROBLEM

I don't have time to do everything! How can I keep up with my children, my housekeeping, my marriage, and a business?

SOLUTIONS FROM SISTER ZOOS

I think it's a good idea to hire a student/teenager or another adult to come in and do the laundry—including the folding and ironing—vacuuming, and picking up; get groceries; wash floors; and/or clean the bathroom. At first it would take a little organization from you to show the person what to do and how you want things done, but in the end it would save your family and your sanity. Check out the book *A Housekeeper Is Cheaper Than a Divorce* by Kathy Fitzgerald Sherman (www.lifetoolspress.com.).

Marilyn C., Alberta

I had a problem finding time for my husband; it seemed like taking care of our marriage was always being pushed to the bottom of our to-do list, which wasn't fair to any of us. We realized that this was causing a problem, so now we actually schedule time each week for just the two of us, and we make sure that we don't skip our "appointments."

Susan N., Iowa

I had trouble keeping up with all the tax filing and paperwork requirements for my business. I hired a bookkeeper, who keeps track of all the details I can't handle. Hiring her was the best decision I ever made.

Sandra P., Georgia

PROBLEM
I can't keep my kids out of my office paperwork.

SOLUTIONS FROM SISTER ZOOS

Designate an office—or even one corner of a room—a no-kid zone, with no exceptions.

Nancy P., California

Have your kids "help" with the paperwork. Break out the workbooks and coloring books. Ask them to keep track of their papers and file them in their own file cabinet. And lock your file cabinet when you are not working.

Calissa L., Florida

Give everyone in your home his or her own space, even if it's just a corner of a room. Teach everyone to respect each other's property. Show them your space and remind them daily that they are not to touch it under any circumstances. And show them how by continuously respecting their space too.

Mia C., Wisconsin

I keep all my important paperwork locked away in the filing cabinet.

Val S., Washington

My workspace is off-limits, but nearby I have a desk with office supplies and a computer for my kids to play "office" while I'm on the computer. They have to understand that most things in Mommy's office are "no touch," but they are welcome to use the other desk, tape, pens, papers, envelopes, and so on for play.

April G., Washington

PROBLEM

My family and friends don't take my business seriously. They think I'm home playing around all day.

SOLUTIONS FROM SISTER ZOOS

Either you can resolve not to care or you can change their perceptions with your own attitude and actions. Take your own business very seriously. Get business cards made up, set working hours, and most of all, make the most of your work time. If they see you running errands and playing all day, it may be hard for them to understand. If you need to, explain how your business is structured (perhaps you work mainly when the kids are sleeping), so your words support your actions.

Nancy P., California

We've all heard this. Just wait until they call you one day and you say, "I'm busy with a client. I'll call you back later!"

Calissa L., Florida

There is no quick fix to this problem. It may take some time before your family and friends take your business seriously. Try to talk about your accomplishments when with them. I had a family member who did not take my business seriously until one day I proudly told her that I had landed my first corporate account. I went into detail about how I got it, and I think for the first time she realized how much work I actually do in my business.

Rachael H., Florida

Make good use of your answering machine. Let it field your calls during business hours. Don't answer the door if anyone you're not expecting stops by. On a daily basis, remind folks whenever you can that you're working and that your time is limited.

Mia C., Wisconsin

The best revenge is the take-home pay. When family and friends see how much money you make at your work, they will take it more seriously. And remember . . . sometimes you get treated the way you allow people to treat you. Learn to say no when people ask you to do things that you normally wouldn't do if you worked away from home.

Alanna W., Oklahoma

My friends, as well as my husband and my children, took me seriously. It was my own mother who didn't take me seriously until I showed her some of my completed projects. It just takes more time for some people than others.

Beth T., New Hampshire

I receive calls from my friends and family and also my husband's family asking if they can come over so I help them learn about the Internet or teach them how to use a program. After all, as far as they're concerned, I just goof around on the Internet all day. What I do now is hand out my business card after each visit. When I do, I tell them very nicely that this time was on me and I'll be sure to give them a nice discount on their next visit. It required a few times before some of them took me seriously, but being persistent actually worked! Now my husband is pitching the idea of my doing a Web site for his company.

Michelle M., California

Invite them to your house. They will definitely see how well you balance work, kids, work, house, work, husband, work. . . .

April G., Washington

Your home business is doing great—don't keep the good news to yourself. It's time to tell the world!

Tooting Your Own Horn

Promoting Your Business, Promoting Yourself

OH, @$&%*

I keep telling my husband that he has to set a good example for our kids. It's not that I'm trying to change him; I really don't care what he says around me. But when our four-year-old daughter said, "Mom, there's way too much crap in my room." I knew something had to be done. It was a simple request. Just replace cuss words with something a little tamer.

"So, when I hammer my thumb, what am I supposed to say?" he asked.

"Oopsie," I told him.

It took quite some time for him to get used to saying "shucks" or "darn" instead of "&%@#*," but he got the hang of it, and before long it was second nature. He'd drop a glass in the kitchen: "Oopsie!" he'd say. Our daughter's vocabulary remained age-appropriate and I was happy. Until one day after he came home from work.

"Cheryl, I've never been so humiliated. Everyone at work is making fun of me now," he told me.

"What happened?"

"I spilled coffee in my lap during a meeting at work. Which was bad enough. But then I said, 'Oopsie.'"

His coworkers couldn't believe their ears. They made him repeat it.

"What did you just say?" they asked.

"Oopsie," he replied sheepishly.

"Oh, everyone got a big kick out of it."

Poor Mike. So I guess the trick is choosing our words a little more carefully. And I've learned that families all have different levels of comfort with their words. I was driving my daughter and her friend Christie in our car one day. They were talking about things they used to say when they were "little."

"When I was little and I farted," my daughter said, "I used to say, 'Oops, my butt burped.'"

"Cheryl!" Christie said, "Dani said a bad word, she said *fart*! That's a bad word in our house, we say toot."

"Well, sorry Christie, but you'll just have to get used to it. *Fart* isn't a bad word at our house." After all, I can only expect my husband to change so much. I mean, please, can you imagine how humiliating it would be for him to say, "Oh, excuse me, I tooted" or, even worse, "My butt burped," if he had an embarrassing moment at work? I just have to draw the line somewhere.

However, there is one kind of tooting that I've had to get used to, and that's tooting my own horn. If promoting yourself makes you uncomfortable, it's time you got used to it too. No one will find out about your business if you don't take the initiative.

Business owners are often surprised to find that their office setup is perfect, they're organized, and everything is in place to start filling orders . . . only the phone is not ringing and customers are not lining up to purchase their products. You have to get out there and let people know what you're doing or you will never make a sale.

The exact words you use to deliver your message are up to you.

YOU SUCK AT THIS

I was at our community pool last summer, watching my daughter jump off the diving board. There was a swim meet going on right next to us. The stands were filled with cheering parents. Jenny's family was sitting next to me. I knew this because I heard them all yelling: "Go, Jenny!" "You can do it, Jenny!" and "Jenny, you rock!" Then the youngest of the group shouted out, "Jenny! You suck at this!"

The stands fell silent. The little girl innocently looked at her mom and said, "What? That's what all the kids say."

I really think that she thought she was yelling encouragement to her big sister. Of course, "You suck at this" doesn't do much to encourage anyone. But sometimes encouragement does come from unexpected sources. How many times have you been spurred to do your best just because someone told you it couldn't be done? Every now and then I hear from a work-at-home mom whose husband was less than supportive when she was first starting her business but has since become her greatest advocate.

I know a few moms who have found that their "I'll show him" attitude was just what they needed to spur themselves along. While I can't advocate going against the wishes of one's spouse—we do have to keep our marriages strong, after all—if he's less than enthusiastic, use it to your advantage. More often than not, once these husbands start seeing the cash roll in, they change their tune.

Hey, I'll take encouragement wherever I can get it.

Flashback to seventh-grade gym class. It was mile-run day. Even though I am not, and never have been, a speedy runner, I was determined to do my best. I wouldn't walk and I would make this my fastest run yet. I remember coming around the turn as I finished my first lap. My whole class was cheering. Huh? They couldn't be cheering for me. But there they were, yelling and clapping, jumping up and down. It was as if they had read my mind; they must have sensed my determination. They saw that even though I wasn't the fastest kid at school, I was really giving it my all. It gave me the extra lift I needed to really pour it on. I was running and smiling, waving to my "fans."

Once I got a little closer I realized that the cheers were actually for the girl who was quickly coming up behind me, the fastest miler in the school, who was about to lap me again, finish her run, and set a new school record, just as I was completing my first lap.

I still remember that feeling, the thrill of thinking they were actually cheering for me, and the letdown and embarrassment when I realized the truth. But for a few moments, I had felt that boost of encouragement and realized how powerful it was. I've obviously never forgotten it. Now I either need therapy or I can use the memory to help others. Therapy's expensive, so I try never to pass up a chance to praise someone or give encouragement. I know how much it means to me.

Give encouragement and accept praise whenever possible. To that little girl, "You suck at this" was a compliment. Who knows? Maybe it is.

Realize that as you're out there "tooting your own horn," there will be people who will try to bring you down. Don't let them. Believe in yourself and continue to promote your business. Success is the best revenge.

PROMOTION IDEAS

Self-promotion is not always easy, and it seems to be especially difficult for women. We have been taught that we should be modest and polite, not toot our own horns. Well, without some horn tooting, no one will know about your business. These tips will help you overcome your reluctance and announce your business to the world.

- Use e-mail to promote your business. Don't send unsolicited e-mail to strangers, but you can start with people you know, people who will be pleased to hear about your new endeavor. Ask them to forward the information to anyone they know who might be interested.
- Become an online expert. Set up your own business Web site and feature articles you've written about your business. For example, if you have an interior design business, post articles about how to find a decorator who matches your personality or decorate on a budget. Since other Web sites are always looking for good content, many will publish your articles. For payment, they will print a bio paragraph about you with a link to your Web site. If it's not obvious how to submit to a site, write to the publisher and ask if the site is open to receiving e-mail submissions. There are other sites that bring together writers and publishers who are looking for content. For example, Idea Marketers at www.ideamarketers.com is used by publishers when they're searching for subject-specific content. Their service is free to writers. You just post your writing and publishers contact you when they want to use your article.
- If you have a Web site for your business, offer reciprocal links to other related sites. You will provide relevant links to your visitors and those links' visitors will be able to find you and your business. This way you can work together with other sites to increase the traffic to all your sites.
- Attend a convention or trade show geared to your target

market. Not only will you meet potential customers, you will also meet other businesspeople with whom you can network as you grow your business.

- Create a speech or presentation for area community groups. You will be providing them with valuable information and you will get more recognition (and publicity) for your business. Be sure to promote the appearance on your Web site and in the local paper.

- Join your chamber of commerce or other small-business organizations to network and work with other business owners.

- Use SCORE, the Service Corps of Retired Executives. SCORE is a nonprofit association of retired executives and former small-business owners who volunteer their time. They are dedicated to entrepreneur education and the formation, growth, and success of small businesses nationwide. Volunteers offer free counseling to business owners and now they even offer e-mail counseling. Find a chapter near you through their Web site at www.score.org or call 800-634-0245.

When you follow these tips, your phone should start ringing!

Using Press Releases to Promote Your Business

Press releases are among the best ways to get recognition for your business without spending a lot of money.

Journalists are always looking for human-interest stories and stories about new businesses in the community. By sending your information to them, you're making their job easier. But you should be aware that hundreds of press releases are sent to news professionals every day. You need an angle that will make your release stand out from the rest.

The following guidelines can help you find and use that angle.

- First of all, press releases should be newsworthy. Watch, read, and listen to the news. Is there a hot topic currently in the news relating to your business? For example, if there are stories about high gasoline prices, focus your story on the money-saving alternative to commuting: working at home. There are ways to position your ideas to make even a simple story into a news story.

- Pay attention to the editor or producer who works on stories related to your subject. If you can't find the appropriate contact person, call and ask to whom you should address your press release. If you are sending your release to coincide with a holiday or certain time of year, send it several weeks in advance of the date.

- Your release may be run without any further contact from the newspaper, or, if the reporter has questions, he or she may contact you for more information or to schedule an interview. If and when someone from the press contacts you, be prepared to talk about your business. Newspeople work with tight deadlines in hectic environments. Don't waste their time. Practice your answers, and always speak with enthusiasm about your business.

- Also consider taking a community college or public information class on public relations. If you have PR money in your budget, hire a PR professional or barter with a PR WAHM. Getting the details right can make the difference in whether your story ends up in the wastebasket or in the newspaper.

PRESS RELEASE TEMPLATE

Here's a press release that I've had success with. You can customize it with your own information and use it to promote your business. Some basic things to remember when drafting an effective press release are

- Incorporate bulleted points. When appropriate, explain the take-away value for your audience in a quick, clear way.

- Make sure your opening paragraph is snazzy and intriguing but also clear as to its purpose.

- Don't overhype. Be realistic, otherwise the media won't take you seriously. If you are promoting your cookie business, you don't need to claim that you are the next Mrs. Fields. Unless, of course, you are about to go public.

- Figure out the focus. In the sample below, the focus is the stay-at-home day, not my business, though WAHM.com is an element. Stay true to your focus.

Sample Press Release

FOR IMMEDIATE RELEASE (Designate whether your information is for immediate release or should be held for a specific date.)

DATE

CONTACT INFORMATION (Include all your contact information in this section. Be sure to include your Web site address, e-mail address, and phone number. You want to be easy to reach.)

Cheryl Demas

Cheryl@WAHM.com

916-985-2078

http://www.wahm.com

STAY HOME WITH YOUR KIDS DAY

Local home-based businesswoman [your name here] is preparing to celebrate the seventh annual "Stay Home With Your Kids Day" on Monday, August 18, 2003. Stay Home With Your Kids Day is sponsored by WAHM.com—The Online Magazine for Work-at-Home Moms. The purpose of the occasion is to provide a day of recognition and celebration for those parents who have chosen to be home with their children.

Cheryl Demas, publisher of the WAHM.com Web site, says, "If you're thinking about leaving the traditional workplace, Stay Home With Your Kids Day is the perfect opportunity to take a vacation day and give serious thought to making the change. Leaving your job may not be an easy decision, but if your heart aches every time you drive away from the child-care center in the morning, it might be time to look at other options." And there are many options for parents today, aside from working full-time outside the home. Many parents are finding that working from home is the perfect solution to their work/home dilemma.

[Your name here] has been running [your business here] from her home since [date] (Enter additional information about your business, and/or a quote about your feelings about being a WAHM here.)

As Demas states, "If we can have a day to take our children to work, we should be able to devote one day to staying home with our children. While we realize that not all parents can or wish to be home full-time with their kids, WAHM.com is dedicated to giving advice and support to those who are determined to make it work. Give it a try; 'mom' can be the best job description you've ever had."

(Indicates the end of your press release)

PROBLEM

I'm really shy. I'm having trouble promoting my business; what can I do?

SOLUTIONS FROM SISTER ZOOS

If you're really shy, an online business is a good choice for you. It's easier to communicate when you don't have to face someone in person. You can be more aggressive in your marketing efforts when your communication is through e-mail, faxes, and Web pages.

Alanna W., Oklahoma

When you're at the grocery store, make sure your baby is in the cart. Babies break the ice and make it easier to strike up a conversation. It has worked wonders for me!

Jennifer M., Ohio

You might want to think of hiring someone to do this part for you, once you've acquired some kind of client base on your own. If you want to be successful, you'll have to break out of your shyness to some degree. It's hard, especially when you have to "toot your own horn," but it's all part of it.

Mia C., Wisconsin

I started out selling my products to family and friends, and everyone was more than glad to place an order to help out at first. Promoting my business has been simple: I put a large sign out in front of my home and a magnetic sign on my truck. I put flyers and business cards up in the stores; I leave catalogs. These methods will help people find out about your business.

Kelly S., Michigan

Check into publicists, use your computer, post your business cards or flyer about your business in supermarkets, libraries, and such places.

Rose Marie B., New York

Join local civic groups, business organizations, and your chamber of commerce. Everyone is there for the same reason, so you shouldn't feel uncomfortable when you're talking about your business.

Val S., Washington

Your home now holds a little something extra that not many homes have . . . a business. It's going to take a little creativity to make it all work.

8

Zoo Maintenance

When My House Is Clean, I Think I'm in the Wrong House

SETTING UP YOUR HOME OFFICE

Depending on the business you choose, you may have to buy a little or a lot of office equipment to get started. You can make your home-office environment as personal as you wish, and you will want to make it flexible. Home-business owners are often given the advice to completely separate their work and home spaces. However, this arrangement isn't always satisfactory for work-at-home moms. I hear from many moms who started out assuming they wanted their office set up in an isolated part of the house, only to find out later that they would rather have their computer in the center of the household activity. Time will tell what works best for you.

Many business owners are tempted to overspend in this phase. They want the latest technology, the most modern office furniture, the best business stationery, and the nicest business cards. Be careful that you don't spend all your profits before you earn them. Two small filing cabinets with a board placed over them can be a functional desk. Of course, you will probably need to buy some supplies: pens, bulletin board, maybe a cordless phone; just don't go overboard. Figure out the minimum that you need to spend to get started, and budget for the things you would like to add as you start making a profit.

Your accountant can help you figure out what supplies you can write off on your taxes and what is the best way to structure your office space in regard to the home-office tax deduction. It is a good idea to consult with him or her before you make any major home-office purchases.

Many work-at-home moms also set up an office space for their children. Check secondhand and consignment shops for used desks,

easels, and even an old-fashioned typewriter. We bought our type-writer on eBay and my kids love it. Dani says the neatest thing is that her words come out on the paper right away. She doesn't have to type and then send it to a printer. She thinks it's high-tech. Children often like working alongside Mom, and it helps establish good organization habits for them too.

Your car can serve as your field office. You can carry product samples and paperwork; when you find yourself waiting to pick up your children from school or sports practices, you can use the time to your advantage. If you organize it carefully, you can work quite efficiently from your car. Many WAHMs use different-color plastic bins or baskets to keep their supplies and paperwork organized in their cars. We also like the seat-back organizers, which attach to the rear of the front seats, to hold children's markers, pencils, papers, and games.

A WAHM I know who sells children's books always has a supply of books in her trunk. The parents at her children's school look for her when they need to buy a birthday gift or just want to see her new products. Because she's organized and always has products with her, she makes many sales from the trunk of her car. You can buy magnetic signs or vinyl letters that attach to your car so you can advertise your business whenever you're on the road. You can also use your car time to listen to motivational and/or educational audiotapes. Your car can become an extension of your home office.

When you work at home, you have the power to choose your work environment. You can make it as traditional or unique as you wish. Because, above all, it's your business!

WHERE ARE MY SOCKS?

I see the lights coming on in all the other houses in my neighborhood and I imagine what their occupants' lives are like. The children awaken to their own alarm clock—no sense waking Mom—and pick out an outfit from their drawers that they have stocked from their color-coded clothes hampers that were filled by Dad the night before . . . even though, according to the color-coded chore chart, it was sister's night to do laundry. But because sister was tired from her night of cooking frozen meals for the homeless shelter, Dad went ahead and did the laundry for her.

Then they grab their bag lunches from the sparkling-clean refrigerator, the lunches that were prepared the night before by brother because according to the color-coded chore chart it was his turn to prepare nutritious lunches for the family for the next day.

The children check their daily planners to make sure all their

homework is complete and that they have any extra items they will need for craft projects or after-school activities.

Mom walks the kids to school and then runs home with her naturally blond hair blowing in the breeze, her trusty golden retriever at her side. Once home, she takes a hot shower and sits down with a cup of herbal tea to plan her day.

I hate them.

Okay, that's what I imagine is going on in their house. I suspect the reality is a little different. And no, I don't really hate them . . . well, maybe just a little.

There's a woman on a TV commercial who says, "When my house is clean, I feel like a better mom." When *my* house is clean, I feel like I'm in the wrong house.

One day my daughter Nicki was playing a game with her friend Emily. Emily gave Nicki clues, trying to get her to say the words *birth certificate.*

Emily said, "Okay, this is something your mom was given as soon as you were born, and she'll keep it with her for the rest of your life."

"Tylenol," Nicki answered.

I'm reminded of this as the kids get dressed every morning. Socks give me a headache.

My favorite thing about summer is that my kids wear sandals every day and they don't need socks. When cooler weather sets in, every morning I hear, "Mom, where are my socks?"

I don't understand why keeping track of socks is so difficult. My husband never understood the problem until I lost my patience one day. "Where do all the socks go? How hard can it be to keep track of socks?" he asked.

"Okay, honey, you want to walk a mile in my shoes?" I put him in charge of socks.

We set up base camp in the hallway so I could acclimate him to

the laundry room. I wouldn't want him to enter such unfamiliar surroundings too quickly. He soon realized that it was an insurmountable challenge and gave up. We're back to "Where are my socks?"

His question, "How hard can it be?" is similar to what I hear from many moms who want to work at home. From the outside, working at home looks like the perfect solution. But just as I suspect that what's going on behind the scenes at my neighbors' houses is a little different from what I imagine, working at home may be different from what you perceive it to be too. Making money, staying at home, taking care of your own kids—it all sounds so good. And it has been a great solution for my family and me, but until you walk in my shoes, don't assume working at home is the perfect solution. A work-at-home mom wears the hats of both a working mother and a stay-at-home mother. And there are no sick days or vacation pay.

Now, I don't presume to understand your situation, and I'll be happy to walk a mile in your shoes too . . . as soon as I find my socks!

Expect the Unexpected

Are you always prepared for the unexpected? If someone wants to visit you at home, do you make excuses or do you let him or her in? Do you run for cover or put out the welcome mat?

You know those lists that rank people's greatest fears? Most often public speaking comes out at the top of the list, but I'm willing to bet that among work-at-home moms, unexpected guests is the greatest fear. I know a lot of work-at-home moms who get stressed out for days when they're expecting visitors.

But what are we stressed about? Do we worry that someone will judge us based on the smudges on our windows? Isn't it better to look forward to the friendships we can share? The fun times we can have, and the contacts we can make? Now, I'm not advocating that you completely let the housework slide, just keep it in perspective. I know I can't work at home, take care of my children, and keep a perfect house too. I doubt if many moms can.

Erma Bombeck wrote that if she had her life to live over again, "I would have invited friends over to dinner even if the carpet was stained and the sofa faded. I would have eaten the popcorn in the 'good' living room and worried much less about the dirt when someone wanted to light a fire in the fireplace."

I started out thinking that I could keep a perfect home and that I could present my children to the world as perfect little citizens. I learned early on that that wouldn't be possible. I had some neighborhood ladies over one day shortly after we had moved into our new house. Nicki was a preschooler and she was sleeping late. When she came downstairs, I thought "Here's where I can impress them with our cheerful morning dialogue."

"Good morning, sweetheart," I greeted her, as Nicki rubbed her eyes. "Did the sandman visit you last night?"

"Yeah, and I think the booger man did too," she answered.

So much for that illusion.

I also used to be more of the run-for-cover type when we had company. If I knew someone was coming over, I would spend hours cleaning and doing my best to get the house close to presentable. Then I would still apologize and say, "I'm so sorry about the state of the house, I just didn't have time to do *any* cleaning before you came." But then either my husband or my kids would come home and blow it by saying, "Whoa, you really cleaned this place up." So now I've decided that it's a WYSIWYG house: What You See Is What You Get. Yes, there are fingerprints on the window (gasp!) and dirty dishes in the sink, and (horrors!) the kids' craft projects are spread over the dining room table . . . but this is just the way it is.

And what a relief it is.

HOUSEKEEPING TIPS

I was surprised when I first started working at home to find that my home was never really being used before, when I was working away from home. Now that I'm managing my home—and my home business—my house is used all the time.

You may find that you care more about your home environment when you're working at home. You work where you live and you live where you work. You don't walk out the door in the morning and come back again at night. Now you are at home all day, and your home is really getting used. But because you're still working, you don't necessarily have more time to devote to housekeeping.

Being a work-at-home mom can also bring up some housekeeping situations that most business people don't have to deal with.

I know a work-at-home mom who was perplexed by a large smudge on all the charge card receipts she ran through her machine, until she discovered a raisin that was squished inside the machine. Another mom was meeting with a client at her home when she discovered that she had sat on a chocolate bar that her child had left on her office chair.

Don't feel that you have to live up to someone else's expectations. You and your family need to work together to find the housekeeping level that works best for you. How much disarray can you live with? Some families insist on keeping at least one area of their home spotless. That way they always have a place where they can entertain guests if someone stops by, without having to clear away clutter. Some moms let things slide during the week and clean like crazy on Saturday morning. Other families do a little each day and have specific daily jobs assigned to each family member. My kids respond best if we limit the cleaning time and set a timer. We break cleaning sessions up into ten-minute intervals, during which everyone pitches in to clean the house. You'd be surprised at how much you can accomplish in a short time if everyone focuses on his or her tasks. Since there's a time limit, my kids are less likely to drag their feet. And since they're so competitive, I also make up cleaning contests. In addition to the timer, we use a stopwatch and time how fast they can get the trash out or empty their hampers. We also keep Barbie barefoot. I don't even try to keep track of her shoes. As soon as she gets out of the box, she says, "My feet are killing me! Get me out of these shoes!" Barbie's much happier that way and so am I.

But most important, when the dishes and laundry and toys are stacked up and you think you can't take it anymore, give your kids a hug, and don't worry about it. Because one day you will look around and the laundry and dirty dishes will still be there, but your kids won't. They will grow up and move on with their lives.

Now if I could just come up with a way to send those Barbie shoes with them.

Cleaning's Not My Thing

My oldest daughter is usually very helpful around the house, but lately she feels ill whenever I ask her to help with cleaning. "You know, Mom," she said the other day, "cleaning just isn't my thing."

Well, it's not my "thing" either, but it still has to be done.

I actually hate cleaning.

I don't know how this family has any hair left on their bodies with all the hair that goes down the drain. I swear I pulled an entire person out of the tub drain one day. And there's nothing I dislike more than cleaning up hair. I'll take cleaning the toilets any day over cleaning up hair. I hate it. I don't understand what it is about hair that makes it so disgusting as soon as it leaves our bodies, but it is awful.

And what happened to that little girl I used to bathe in the kitchen sink? After she takes a shower now, the bathroom is a disaster. The shower curtain is torn, the towel rack is ripped off the wall, wet towels are everywhere, the carpet is soaked, the shampoo is spilled on the floor—it looks like a gorilla has been in the bathroom. No, a gorilla would probably at least pick up his towels.

Now, when Nicki's trying to decide what to wear in the morning, she tries on about ten outfits and tosses them on the floor as she takes them off. Now she has discovered that it is so much easier to gather them all up and throw them in the dirty clothes than to refold them and put them away. I was feeling a great sense of accomplishment one evening, as I had washed all the dirty clothes and completely emptied the laundry hamper. Imagine my surprise the next

morning when I found five pairs of jeans and ten blouses in the hamper. I knew even she couldn't possibly have worn all those clothes in one day!

There was a time when the house stayed clean. Back when Nicki had a Cinderella obsession. We would watch the movie together and then she always wanted to act it out. She gave me the role of the wicked stepmother. I would order her to sweep and mop the floors, and she dutifully did her chores, singing her sad tunes all the while. It was great. My house has never been so clean again.

One of the best-selling housekeeping books has almost nine hundred pages. What can I possibly add to the wealth of information that is already out there? Not much. So I've come up with a little of my own advice. This is real-world, emergency advice. Trust me, you won't hear these tips from the Martha Stewarts of the world.

Every time I get out the vacuum, my daughter asks, "Who's coming over?" Now, come on, it's not like that's the only time I vacuum. Well, maybe I am kind of predictable. If you're entertaining and you have limited time to prepare, you'll have to prioritize your tasks. First of all, consider the height of your guests. Unless you're expecting the Harlem Globetrotters, the dust can stay on top of the refrigerator for now. Your gaggle of average PTA moms won't be able to see higher than the third shelf on the bookshelf anyway, so just don't worry about anything above the first five and half feet or so of your house.

Next, what is their bladder capacity? How long will they be staying? You can use this information to figure out if you need to clean both bathrooms. If someone insists on using the second bathroom, you can just claim it's broken. I know one work-at-home mom who did graphic artwork. One day when a client was visiting at her home office and asked to use her bathroom, she actually sent him down the street to the gas station.

Now don't get me wrong, we do occasionally get caught up with housekeeping, but when I get really busy, things start to slide again. We had company once . . . well, we've actually had company more than once, but this particular time one of my daughters reached under a sofa cushion and pulled out . . . a can of Cheez Whiz! Of course she couldn't discreetly hand it to me, it had to be announced and displayed for all to see. I guess it was funny, and it could have been worse. Heaven knows what's living under those cushions.

After that I decided that it would be a good idea to keep a list of rules handy for guests. I will share my rules with you; feel free to use them as is or adapt them to meet your specific needs.

1. Don't lift any sofa or chair cushions, and for heaven's sake *never* reach under one without looking first.

2. If a door is closed, it's closed for a reason. *Do not* open it.

3. Don't peek behind the shower curtain. It's not pretty and I won't be responsible for post–traumatic stress disorder.

4. Don't open closet doors; they are spring-loaded. Flying debris may injure you, and the doors cannot be shut again without the help of at least three people.

5. Don't venture into the laundry room. The pile of clothes in there is so high that I personally need supplemental oxygen just to reach the hand washables. The last guest that ignored this warning has never been seen again. We sent out a search party, but they had to give up after three days.

I hope these rules will save me from more embarrassing moments and protect my guests from injury. I know everything will get taken care of eventually. I'm willing to accept working conditions that some might consider less than ideal in order to keep working at home. Eventually I'll be making enough money with my business that I can hire the help I need. Until then . . . please pass the Cheez Whiz!

THE PROCRASTINATION PROBLEM

Procrastination is a huge problem for me. In fact, I was going to write a whole chapter about procrastination for this book, but I never got around to it.

It doesn't matter what it is that I have to do; I will find something, anything, to do instead. Lists help me quite a bit, but I have to be constantly aware of my tasks or I slide into my old habits. Like the time I had a big project to finish and I asked my husband if he could take the girls out for a few hours. He agreed to take them out for pizza. The girls were excited by the "Daddy date" and happily waved good-bye. I stood at the door for a minute, listening to, and enjoying, the silence. Then I headed for the computer . . . well, not quite yet: First I'd better put away those dishes, and I might as well throw in a load of laundry.

On my way to the laundry room, I walked by the mirror and noticed that my eyebrows really needed a good plucking. How long has it been since I've had time to do that? And my toes! Wouldn't a nice coat of fresh polish be just the thing for summer?

Now, back to the laundry. . . . Then I saw my daughter's dress that needed mending, which would take just a second. After all, if I didn't get it fixed soon, she would have outgrown it. Then, throw in another load of laundry, and . . . I'd better iron that shirt for tomorrow.

What a great feeling; I was getting so much accomplished.

Then, finally, I sat down at the computer and got ready to really get some work done!

That's when I heard the key in the door. "Mom, we're home!"

Sometimes it's just impossible to do it all. That's when I have to sit down, take a deep breath, and just accept things the way they are. After all, if I can make our home a safe and happy place, a place where my family knows they can come to refresh and regroup, a place where they know they are loved unconditionally, a place where they can "scratch where it itches," as they say, that's what makes me feel like a good mom. And there's no greater gift I can give them.

MY SAUSAGE

Our daughter wanted an extra piece of sausage one morning, so Mike ran back into the fast-food restaurant to get it for her. I expected him to come back with a piece of sausage, but no, he came back with a bag full of food. Instead of ordering one piece of sausage (because it wasn't on the menu), he ordered the Sausage McMuffin with Egg sandwich; only he ordered it without the cheese, egg, or muffin. The worker told him he could get the Sausage McMuffin with Egg meal for only twenty cents more, and then he could get hash browns and coffee too.

Finally he came back to the car and handed the bag to me. As we drove away, I opened the bag to find: coffee, hash browns, muffin, egg, and cheese, but, you guessed it, no sausage!

Is your home business like my breakfast bag? Did you start out with a specific purpose, a goal in mind? Such as working from home so you could spend more time with your children? Have you gradually drifted away from your original purpose? Are you so engrossed in your business that you've lost sight of the reason you started working from home in the first place? I know it's easy, even tempting sometimes, to get so caught up in the day-to-day details of working that we forget to pay attention to the things that are really important in our lives.

I've had plenty of days lately when I've had more work than hours. I sometimes have to remind myself of my priorities and rearrange my schedule so I'm here for the kids and for the things that really matter to me. These moments, the time I have with my husband and girls, the memories we're making together, are my "sausage." This is what I want more than anything else, so I give them priority.

I'd hate to work for years, thinking I'm doing the best for my kids and my family, only to find I've ended up with a bag full of hash browns.

PROBLEM
I don't have room in my house for a home office.

SOLUTIONS FROM SISTER ZOOS
You can work in a closet and store supplies in a cupboard. You don't need a whole office.

Nancy P., California

Dining rooms work wonders! As do bedrooms or living rooms. The dining room table and a couple of kitchen cupboards work well enough as a desk and storage space.

Calissa L., Florida

Get creative. I use the top of my fridge, my cabinets, and a rolling cart. I use colored folders to help store my materials, red for immediate-release items going out, blue for soon to go, yellow for work in progress, green for items on hold, black for rejections, and white for rewrites. I use the inside of the folder to pencil in dates to remind me where, when, and to whom I've sent material.

Rose Marie B., New York

I use a portable room divider to screen off a section of our family room. It works great for us; my office is somewhat private, yet I'm still here for the kids when they need me.

Jennifer S., New York

If you already have a computer, you have an office. Shoeboxes work great for many things and can easily be labeled and placed under beds. How many clothes do you have in your closet that can be given away? Make more room by getting rid of the things you don't need. An organizer on wheels is incredible because it can be moved to the kitchen table or wherever your office has to be that day.

Val S., Washington

PROBLEM
My house is a wreck. How can I keep it reasonably clean?

SOLUTIONS FROM SISTER ZOOS

Promise yourself that once you start making *x* amount, you will hire a cleaning service. If your time is better spent working and you don't have time or energy or desire to clean, this can be one of life's little luxuries.

Nancy P., California

My trick is using "phone time" as "clean time." I have a cordless phone, so quiet tasks, such as folding clothes, dusting, and cleaning off my desk, can be done without offending the person on the other end. I also remind myself that my house was a wreck when I worked forty-plus hours a week outside the home too.

Lynn T., Tennessee

I solved this problem with the barter system. A friend of mine owns a housecleaning service. I offered computer lessons, Web site design, and printing services for her cards and flyers in exchange for housecleaning services once every two weeks. She is happy because her business has picked up and I am happy because I don't cringe when someone arrives unannounced. It's a win-win situation!

Teri F., Texas

I pride myself on having a clean house. I stick to a schedule. I do certain things at certain times of the day. A mess bothers me. I can't cook in my kitchen if there are dishes in the sink! My biggest problem is storage. I never seem to have enough.

I am constantly reorganizing something! My best tips are to stick to a regimented schedule, redo it as necessary, and always make lists of things you need and need to do. I keep a simple three-ring binder with a calendar where I jot down anything that needs doing and look at it daily. If I didn't do this, I would miss all kinds of appointments, school concerts, and scout meetings.

Amanda F., FamilyCorner.com

I have my workstation located between the kitchen and the family room, where I can see everything going on. I know many work-at-home moms view this as a big no-no, but it works for me. The kids can talk to me as they need to—I can see my toddler and my older boys as they play. I tried moving my office into a room off the kitchen that was more isolated, and things just fell to pieces. The kids actually interrupted me more when I had my own space. My advice to work-at-home moms is to do what works for you, even if it's unconventional. Experiment with work space and schedules until you come up with what works.

Brenda H., Michigan, OldFashionedLiving.com

With the extra money you make from your business, you can hire a nearby teenager to come to your home once a week to clean up a little bit.

Calissa L., Florida

Being a work-at-home mom is like having two jobs. You need to schedule time to clean your house, just as you need to schedule time to work your business. Commit to an hour each day to straighten the house and dedicate a day each week to the big jobs, like cleaning your bathroom. Assign smaller chores to children and your spouse. It takes work to juggle the two, but keeping some sort of cleanliness and order to your home will also help your spouse and family to be more supportive of your business.

Rachael H., Florida

Delegate and follow up! Let others in your home know that you're doing something important to better your family and everyone needs to pitch in. Try coming up with a chart sheet so that all the jobs are done each week and nobody has to argue over who's to do what. If it's been a successful week with tasks and chores, treat them to something fun, like a trip out for ice cream.

Mia C., Wisconsin

If you make enough money, spend money on a maid service. Having someone come in once or twice a week can make a big difference. And it might be cheaper than you think.

Alanna W., Oklahoma

Time management is important. Schedule one big task a day, for example: Monday, floors; Tuesday, refrigerator; Wednesday, stove; Thursday, dusting; Friday, polishing; and so on.

Rose Marie B., New York

Keeping your house neat and clean while operating your business from home is just like working outside the home. You need to do it either in the morning, at night, or on the weekends. If there is no use for something, then you need to get rid of it so that everything has a place and you are not constantly moving the things you don't need.

Beth T., New Hampshire

Dedicate ten minutes a day to each room, or pick one room a day to clean. Rotate so that each room gets thoroughly cleaned once a week. Also, dedicate a certain time to housekeeping only. From 7:00 to 9:00 A.M. it's cleaning, kids, breakfast, showers, and so on. From 9:00 to 12:00 it's work; 12:00 to 1:00 is lunch and cleanup. Establish a routine that works for you and your kids.

April G., Washington

When your husband vowed to become your partner for life, he probably didn't think he'd become your business partner too. You may love your business, but can your marriage handle it?

9

Animal Husbandry

Balancing Your Work and Your Marriage

I'm Not a Passenger

My little girl tells me that I'm lucky because I have two seats in the car: "The driving seat, and the helping-Dad-drive seat." Okay, so maybe I have a tiny little control issue. Passenger just isn't a role I fill easily, and I'm a better partner than a subordinate. In fact our first fight occurred when I was in the helping-Dad-drive seat; actually it was the helping-fiancé-drive seat at the time.

We were planning our wedding, driving out to the country to a florist to pick out floral arrangements. I was in my helping seat, giving directions, and I told him to turn at the green house. He saw a greenhouse up ahead and continued driving, right past the green house. So I told him again, only a little louder, "TURN AT THE GREEN HOUSE!" and he told me, "I AM GOING TO."

"HOW CAN YOU? YOU JUST PASSED THE GREEN HOUSE."

"NO I DIDN'T, IT'S RIGHT THERE!"

Thank goodness it didn't take long for us to figure out the source of our confusion or we might never have made it to our wedding day.

Overall, I feel so lucky that I married a man who is my partner in everything, *even* driving. He is my secret to success. I don't know how I could work at home without his support, a sentiment I hear from so many other work-at-home moms.

I hope you have a supportive husband, but if you don't, don't give up. Many things will change when you begin working at home, but don't just assume that your husband will be one of them. Perhaps with a little adjustment in both of your attitudes, he will come around. After all, having a happy wife and family is in his best interest too. Remind your husband that you share the goal of raising your children to become happy, productive adults. He probably agrees that having them cared for by someone who loves them is the best path to that goal. If so, you're halfway there already.

If your husband doesn't support the idea of your working at home, don't make the mistake of assuming that he will change his mind after you start your business. He may come around if and when you start making money with your business, but there are no guarantees.

Make sure he knows how important working at home is to you and your children. When you're first deciding whether to work at home, calculate together where you can cut expenses. Work together as a team on your daily schedules. These will change as you begin your business and as it grows.

Demonstrate to your husband how his life may be easier when you are at home. Perhaps he won't have to leave work early to share pickups and drop-offs at school and child care, or trade sick days with you to care for a sick child. You will be available to do that now. If he travels often on business, it won't be as difficult to coordinate

your work and child-care schedules when he is out of town. Your mornings may be less hectic, since you will have control of your own work schedule and you won't have to hurry your children out of the house to child care.

Establish your expectations with your husband before you begin working at home and continue to communicate with one another as your business grows. Your business isn't worth jeopardizing your relationship for, so be sure that you agree on decisions. Of course there will be ups and downs, but common goals and expectations will make the transition easier.

TAKE YOUR SPOUSE FOR A TEST-DRIVE

When I ask other moms about the secret to their business success, a supportive spouse is almost always at the top of their list. I'm lucky that Mike is so supportive of my business; he is my biggest fan. But there are moments when I wonder if we're really on the same page, or even the same planet. Maybe it's that whole Mars-Venus thing.

My husband has great focus and can really concentrate on the task at hand. However, he concentrates on only one thing at a time. I don't have that luxury; I have to be able to do fifty things at once. I think this is the biggest difference between us. Moms are always being pulled in several directions. You've got your family, your home, and now your home business, all competing for your time and attention. Moms seem to have an amazing ability to do many things at the same time. My husband, on the other hand, concentrates on what interests him. If I'm making lunch and the dog has to go out and the phone is ringing and the kids are arguing . . . Mike will say, "Do you know who the Browns are playing this weekend?"

So why is it that he's able to simultaneously watch two football games, a basketball game, and ESPN's *SportsCenter*? He might not remember where we went on our first date, but he can tell you Bernie Kosar's rookie-season pass-completion statistics without missing a beat. We just have different styles.

I hear from a lot of moms who are frustrated that their husbands don't help out more around the house or help with the children more. Maybe they just have a different way of doing things. Maybe they just get frustrated if they're always being corrected or told that they're not doing things the "right" way. I notice that Mike and I both are most frustrated when I expect him to do things just as I do.

When I really think about it, the differences keep things interesting anyway. So we choose to enjoy the differences and use them to our advantage. A marriage is a partnership, and we both need to take on different roles from time to time.

For example, Mike loves to shop for cars, and the girls love to accompany him on the shopping trips. Now that's not how I would choose to entertain them, but if it works for them, why not? We get Christmas cards from car salesmen. He walks into a dealership, and he's like Norm on *Cheers*. "Mike!" they shout. Everybody knows his name. We're always getting phone calls from salesmen: "Is Mike still thinking about that Mustang?" they'll ask.

"Mustang? What Mustang?" I can always tell where he's been the night before by which car dealers call the next day.

The other night he called home from across town to tell me he was going to be late.

"Cheryl, the traffic is horrible. It was taking forever to get home. I was so tired of driving, I just had to stop and do something. Then I remembered that there's a Ford dealer in this part of town. So I stopped to check out their inventory."

"Wait, let me guess, you went for a test-drive?"

"Right. How did you know?"

"You do realize how absurd that is, don't you?" I asked him. "You were so tired of driving, you stopped for a test-drive?"

"Well, yeah, but I was driving a different car."

"Like that makes a difference."

The girls have spent wonderful evenings with their dad playing games, reading books, watching movies, and going for test-drives, while I'm able to work uninterrupted. No, he doesn't do things exactly as I would, but as long as there are no trips to the emergency room, I'm happy.

WHAT'S SO FUNNY?

I used to have a huge problem with public speaking. I would do anything to avoid having to speak before a group. It terrified me. I would even get nervous talking to myself in the mirror. When I had to take speech class in college, I avoided it until the last possible semester.

Then it was either take the class or not graduate. I was a wreck during my first speech; I could barely stand and speak at the same time. So I went to my teacher for advice. I expected him to give me some "picture them in their underwear" type of advice. But no, he recommended that I have one or two shots of whiskey before class. And that was an 8:00 A.M. class! That's how bad I was. I don't remember much of the class after that, but I passed, so I must have done okay.

Our move to California finally gave me an opportunity to try to overcome this obstacle. I realized that if I was going to have a successful business, it was time to get over my fear of public speaking. I had heard great things about Toastmasters from several people, so I found a local group and joined. If you suffer from the same affliction, don't wait another minute. Find a Toastmasters group today. They are wonderful.

It wasn't easy, and the change didn't happen overnight, but with the help of my Toastmasters group, my nerves eventually settled down. They guided me along and they didn't even recommend alcohol. After a year, I entered the Toastmaster's humorous-speech contest. I had written a short speech about our wacky family, and it wasn't too bad, if I say so myself. I won at my club level, I won the district; one more level to go and I would go to the state competition. I was thrilled.

The night of the regional contest, the whole family was in the audience. As I delivered my speech, I noticed Mike in the back of the room. He was sitting with his arms crossed, stone-faced. Not so much as a grin or a smirk. Remember, this was a humorous-speech contest, my speech was supposed to be funny, he should have been laughing. What was I doing wrong? After my speech, I asked him, "Why weren't you laughing?"

"I heard it all before. I was there, remember?"

"Well, you could have faked it," I told him.

Then the next contestant took the stage. I don't even remember the subject of his speech; it was dating or something. What I do remember is my husband's reaction. That speech killed him. He was holding his stomach, wiping away tears. And when my husband laughs, the whole room laughs with him. You can't help yourself. The guy's speech was funny, just not *that* funny. But Mike doesn't hold his laughter only for hilarious material; if he's in a good mood, he's laughing. And something must have happened between my speech and the next contestant's to put him in a *great* mood.

I tried to shoot him a look and hint that he wasn't exactly helping my cause.

"*Mike! Shut up!*" I mouthed.

But he didn't stop. At the beginning of the speech, Mike was the only one laughing. By the end, the whole room was roaring.

"What were you doing in there?" I asked him as we waited outside while the judges totaled their votes.

"What? It was funny. What was I supposed to do?"

I don't have to tell you who won the contest. I really was happy with second place, and I'd hate to be a poor loser. The winner's speech *was* funny, and I was happy for him. I hope Mike was happy for him too, because he had all night on the couch to think about it.

QUALITY TIME

It's not easy to find quality time with your husband with little ones underfoot, and it's even more difficult when you're working at home. Your business creates one more distraction, one more thing that's vying for your attention.

One creative work-at-home mom I know managed to arrange some intimate time with her husband by telling the kids that Mom and Dad had to go downstairs to "fix the dryer." She did have to do some fast talking though, when the kids had a private phone conversation with Grandma and asked her if she had any extra money she could send them. They explained that Mom and Dad needed the money for a new dryer because "Grandma, our dryer is *always* breaking, and when Mom and Dad go downstairs to fix it, they lock the door and they don't even let us watch!"

Her mother-in-law was understanding. "Do you know what your kids just asked me for?" she asked my friend when she got her on the phone. Of course the mom was mortified. "Don't worry, honey, I understand. When my husband and I were younger, we had the same problem with our water heater."

Devoting time to your marriage is just as important as taking care of yourself and your children. Be careful that you don't put your relationship with your spouse on the back burner. Schedule time together and stick to it, and keep that clothes dryer in good repair.

What Did You Say?

I know that some women complain that their husbands never listen to anything they have to say. I don't have that problem. It might actually be easier for me if my husband just didn't listen at all. But no, he always listens; he just doesn't hear me sometimes. Some time back I was feeling philosophical and was telling him about how I was going to do my best to put only positive energy into the world. If someone cut me off in traffic or gave me a dirty look or cut in front of me at the grocery store, I'd smile at the person. "Because, you see," I told him, "to do anything else would only put negative energy into the universe. And the universe doesn't need any more negative energy."

I was getting all Oprah on him, and as he usually does when I go Oprah, his eyes glazed over. He was listening; he just didn't really hear everything I said. But he just nodded and smiled and agreed with me, which normally is a very good strategy for him to follow. The only time I get in trouble is when he repeats what he thinks he heard.

Several days later I had time to chat with one of his coworkers. "I hear you're a writer," she said. "Mike told me about your theory of having positive energy in your uterus. Good for you. I think it is so important for women to realize that power." Thinking she had me figured for an earth-mother type—full of energy from my uterus—I just nodded and smiled.

"Yes, that's very important," I agreed.

When I was alone with my husband again, I asked him, "When did I ever tell you anything about energy in my uterus?"

"You remember, when you said how you were going to smile at people at the store from now on," he said.

"Oh, good God. I said I was going to stop putting negative energy into the *universe,* not my *uterus*!"

"See, there you go. You're putting out a lot of negative energy right now. That's not doing either of us any good, is it?" He responded.

I hate it when he throws my own theories back at me.

I have to keep reminding myself that Mike and I have different communication styles, and if I want him to continue to support my business, I have to continue to communicate with him. And I can't assume that he is hearing the same message that I think I'm giving him. I may need to tell him about a frustrating customer or a computer crash just because I need to get it off my chest. But he might assume that I'm bringing my problems to him, looking for a solution. Careful, constant communication is so important in any marriage, and especially important when you're working at home. Don't get lazy in your marriage communication—or you just might end up with a uterus full of negative energy.

I Can't Tell a Lie

Kids keep you honest. I'm basically a very honest person, but every now and then there's a little something that happens and I have to tell the girls, "Now, we don't have to tell Dad about this. I'm not saying to lie, but if he doesn't ask, we don't *have* to tell him this happened." Which, of course, is a big mistake because then both of them race to be the first one to spill the beans to their dad.

They do try sometimes though. Once there was a stray dog in our neighborhood, and of course I just couldn't leave it running in the streets. So we brought it home and put it in the backyard with our dog, Alice, until we could find the owners. I told the kids, "I will tell Daddy about this, but let's wait until he gets home so he can see for himself how cute the dog is and he won't get upset about it before he even sees it." So later that day when my husband called, Nicki answered the phone.

"How is everything going, Nicki?"

"Just fine, Dad. Alice is outside, and there are no other dogs on the deck. Just Alice. Just our dog. One dog on the deck."

"Let me talk to Mom."

Another time they did a little better, managing to keep quiet until they thought that the deception had gone too far.

I don't like confrontation, and I don't like arguing, so when election time rolls around I pretty much agree with my husband. In the 1996 presidential election, we agreed that we would both vote for Ross Perot. But at the poll, Nicki was at my side as I punched my card for another candidate. I was hoping she wouldn't notice. No such luck. Believe me, there would have been no hanging chads in the 2000 election if my daughter had been standing alongside every Florida voter. She went over my ballot as if her life depended on it.

"Mom! Do you realize what you just did?" she gasped.

"Yes, Nicki, I know who I voted for, and we don't have to tell Dad about this."

We rode home in silence, and I waited for her to spill the beans at dinner that night. She remained silent. Weeks went by and I thought I had gotten away with it. Until one day when Mike was on the phone with his mother.

"Cheryl and I both voted for Perot," he told her.

"Oh no you didn't!" Nicki chimed in.

"I'm sorry, Mom, I tried." She told me later. "It was different when it was just in the family, but he was telling Grandma. You can't lie to *Grandma!*"

So they keep me honest, which is good, and I don't keep anything from my husband anymore; it places too much burden on the kids.

But now I don't let him get away with anything either.

My husband loves to tell stories, but he has a habit of embellishing them, just a little. He says it makes them more interesting. When we were first married, I just couldn't let him get away with any inaccuracy. I would constantly correct and qualify his facts so he wouldn't mislead anyone. One day my dad pulled me aside and recommended that I just let Mike go and not constantly correct him. Realizing the error of my ways, I agreed. So I vowed that the next time Mike got rolling with one of his stories, I would just let him go.

A few nights later, we were out to dinner with a group of friends. We were talking about the Minnesota State Fair (famous for various foods on a stick). All our friends agreed that their favorite fair food was the deep-fried cheese curds. Mike and I had talked about making them at home, but we hadn't actually done it yet. But away he went anyway, believing that telling how we were *thinking* about making homemade deep-fried cheese curds wouldn't be much of a story, so he told everyone that we had made them at home ourselves.

I could see him glance my way, and emboldened by my silence, he continued. "They were delicious! Better than the fair! And so easy." Now the crowd was interested.

"How did you do it?" they asked.

I sat back. "I'll just let him dig a hole for himself," I thought. He kept going.

"We used our little deep fryer, got curds from the cheese shop, mixed a batch of batter, and that's all there was to it. They were so much better than the curds at the fair."

"How did you make the batter?" they wanted to know.

"We used a mix," he answered.

Not bad; I had to admit I was impressed with his improvisation. I just smiled and nodded. He was definitely on a roll.

"Where did you buy the batter mix?"

He hesitated. I thought they had him on this one. I smiled. Then he played his trump card. "I don't know, Cheryl bought it. Where did you get that mix, honey?"

Oh, my God. I was in too deep to deny the story now. I had gone along with his lies, and now he had wrapped me up in his web of deceit. I had no choice but to continue the deception.

"I just bought batter mix at the grocery store." I muttered.

We went straight home and made fried cheese curds that night, and I've never gone along with another story since then.

You might be tempted to embellish when you're asked to take on a project that you're not quite capable of doing. I've heard from many women who got in over their heads when they said, "Sure, I can do that."

I know a work-at-home mom who was offered a contract to do promotional work for a client. She completed the work, but neither she nor the client was happy with the results. She later admitted that she had underestimated the amount of time the job would take and exaggerated her relationships with media contacts in the community. It didn't take long for her to realize that she was in over her head.

It's one thing to tell a tall cheese-curd tale to a group of friends (or a voting fib to your husband) and another thing to be dishonest in your business dealings. When your professional reputation has been damaged, it takes more than some fried cheese curds to restore it.

The Way to My Heart Is through My Washing Machine

Husbands of America, listen to what I'm telling you. The sexiest thing a man can do is housework. I hear from a lot of women, and trust me on this one. The women who really talk glowingly about their husbands don't brag about his skills in the boardroom or bedroom, it's the laundry room that really does it for them. I saw a sign at a gift shop once that said, "No husband has ever been shot while doing the dishes." I'm sure that's true. I had one WAHM.com reader tell me that she has her husband dress in a thong when he vacuums and dusts. Can you imagine? Here's a tip for Chippendales—if you want to appeal to the "mature" women in your audience, have your men add a little dusting to their dancing. They'll get so many dollar bills they'll be able to retire.

On the other hand, if you really want to start a fight with your wife, come home from work, shake your head, and then say in a snide voice, "What did you do all day?"

A friend of mine has a laundry system that works for her. She has limited space, so she has "stations" for her laundry as it goes through various stages. As she folds the clean laundry, she stacks it on a dining room chair, and then when she gets a couple of loads finished, she puts away the folded clothes. So there's always a batch of folded clothes on the chair, as they're rotating through the laundry cycle. Apparently her husband had noticed the stack of folded clothes but never paid that much attention to them, until one day he came home and put away the stack of clothes. His wife was pleased; she thanked him and he said, "Well, they've been sitting there for six months, I figured you'd *never* put them away, so if I didn't do it they'd sit there forever."

She wasn't quite so pleased after that.

From time to time I have dreams about my husband in which he does something horrible. One night my dream husband traded our van in on a motorcycle. He told me I could ride in the sidecar. Another night he threw my antique quilts in the garbage and hung black-velvet paintings throughout the house. Those dreams seemed so real to me that I woke up still feeling angry with him. The feelings of anger held over, well into the waking hours of the morning. Poor Mike. He hadn't really done anything wrong, yet he ended up bearing the brunt of my bad mood for the entire morning.

But the other morning I woke up feeling *extremely* affectionate toward my husband. I had dreamed about him again, and in my

dream he was doing the dishes. That was it, very simple, no complicated symbolism, he just did the dishes. The feelings I had for him in
this dream also carried over into my waking hours. He was pleased
with the attention, because after this many years of marriage, I don't
wake up feeling *that* happy with him very often.

I finally told him the source of my pleasure. "Honey," I whispered, "last night . . . I dreamed . . . that you did the dishes."

I was watching a movie the other day and there was a scene that
featured a man in a bathtub. A bare-naked man in a bathtub. As I was
watching it, I was turned on, excited—no, not because of the man in
the tub—I was excited because that grout was so *white*. How did they
do it? I'm not kidding, it was sparkling. Hollywood has found yet
another way to mess with my mind and make me feel inadequate.

What has become of me? There was a time when the bare-naked
man in the tub would have been what caught my attention, and it used
to take at least a *little* romance to put me in the mood. Now all it takes
is an imaginary cupboard full of clean dishes. Instead of jewelry, I'm
enticed by the illusion of a clean kitchen. Apparently a stack of folded
laundry or an empty sink is as satisfying as a candlelit dinner.

I suspect my husband will never willingly do many domestic
chores. However, I did notice a change after that dream morning. He
did the dishes every day that week.

SHY HOUSEKEEPER SYNDROME

They say that there are two things you should never watch, laws or
sausage being made. Apparently there's a third item: your husband
doing housework. Unless he's in a thong, of course.

Seriously, occasionally my husband will have a burst of energy
and tackle a big housekeeping project. He'll clean out the refrigerator or organize the closets. Recently I realized that I have never actu-

ally witnessed any of these activities. His bursts of energy always happen when I'm away from home. I have never, ever seen him vacuum. This leads to two possible conclusions: (1) he's not actually doing the work himself but is hiring someone to come in when I'm away from home, or (2) for some reason he can do housework only when I'm not watching.

He claims the answer is no. 2. He says if I saw how he does housework, I would "freak out." He says that like the creation of laws and sausages, the act of him doing housework is not something I would want to witness. I'll take my chances. I'll risk a little freak-out to get some help around here.

I'm not buying it though. I believe I've identified a new disorder, Shy Housekeeper Syndrome. Those afflicted with SHS are unable to clean, straighten, pick up, wash . . . anything . . . if someone is watching. The poor SHS sufferers struggle with their desire to do housework; they just can't bring themselves to do it.

As therapy, I recommend that SHS sufferers start small: pick up a pair of socks, put a bowl in the dishwasher. Who knows, you might even work your way up to throwing in a load of wash one day.

I say, give it a try. I'm sure your spouse will be supportive. I know I'm willing to risk "freaking out" in exchange for a little housecleaning.

PROBLEM

My husband does not support my business.

SOLUTIONS FROM SISTER ZOOS

This is a big issue, and you and your husband need to have some heart-to-heart talks about why this is. You might want to seek the assistance of a counselor to help you both understand what the issue is here and how to resolve it. Without your husband's support, either your business or your relationship is bound for trouble.

Nancy P., California

Some husbands don't believe that home businesses can be successful. Once you start making some extra money, treat him to a night out or a new TV and let him know where the money came from.

Calissa L., Florida

At first my husband didn't really take my business seriously either but saw it more as a hobby. Because our boys were having so much fun with the toys (and we were too), my husband just thought it was an investment in family togetherness. As my business grew and I began receiving calls from customers and the UPS truck visited our house regularly, my husband's attitude began to change.

The real turning point, however, came one day when he saw a stack of cash and checks on our counter. "Where did we get all this?" he asked, very surprised. I just smiled and told him I was working on making a deposit to my Discovery Toys checking account. His answer? *Wow!*

Katherine G., Virginia

This is a very tough one. There's not much you can do to change your husband, but you can demonstrate your seriousness and prove to him that your time away from him is worthwhile when your first customer rolls in! In time he'll see the fruits of your labor, as long as he doesn't feel that he's lost you to your business.

Mia C., Wisconsin

Your husband may support you when he begins to see a pay-check. Mine wasn't so supportive either, especially given the monthly expenses (Internet access, separate phone line, and so on), but once he saw that I was making up to one thousand dollars a week, he sure changed his opinion. And he really started pitching in with the dishes, laundry, and other household chores. He just needed to see that it was paying off.

April G., Washington

Okay, now you've got your husband on your side, it's time to bring your children onboard the home-business bandwagon too.

10

Welcome to the Monkey House

Working with Children

IT'S A MOM THING

I have tried in the past to explain to childless friends why I left a good, high-paying job to work at home, to stay at home with my kids. I've never really felt that I could adequately describe the reasons I want to be home with my girls. I've never felt that I had successfully convinced anyone that I'm doing what I really want to do. They still seem to think that I'm sacrificing something, or missing out, just so I don't have to put my kids in child care.

A few years ago my daughter made a huge tissue paper Mother's Day carnation corsage for me. She presented it to me on Mother's Day morning, and of course expected that I would wear it all day. And I did. I wore it to church, to breakfast, to the mall. From other mothers I received smiles and knowing glances; from nonmothers, I received stares and curious looks. I could tell they were wondering what would possess me to attach several square feet of multicolored tissue paper to my chest. I overheard one of the young salesclerks at the mall say to a colleague as they walked away, "It must be a mom thing."

I knew they could never understand, so I didn't even try to explain. But after I thought about it, I decided she was right. It is a "mom thing." Before I was a mom, there was no way I could have understood it either.

WHERE'S BUDDY?

I made one of the biggest mistakes of my mothering career when Nicki was about three years old. I picked up her favorite teddy bear and gave him a voice. He talked to her at bedtime every night after that. When she was sad or scared, she would talk to Buddy and tell him things she would never say to me directly. Buddy went everywhere with her. When she was first diagnosed with diabetes, he was the only thing she packed to take to the hospital with her.

As Nicki got older, Buddy still went everywhere with her. Not so much as her "security blanket" anymore but as a piece of her childhood that continued to be a part of her life. She took pictures of him at national landmarks and made a scrapbook with pictures of all the places Buddy had visited. He was a well-traveled bear. He saw Mount Rushmore, Old Faithful, Las Vegas, Hollywood; he really got around.

I said giving him a voice was a mistake because giving Buddy a personality gave him life. And as with all living things, his life must someday come to an end. Buddy seems to have met his end in a dark parking lot on Christmas night in Mojave, California. Through what we've been able to piece together, he fell out of our van when we stopped for gas on our way to Arizona.

My daughter turned fifteen the next day. Too old for a bear, I guess, but Buddy had become more than just a stuffed animal. He was our communication pathway, a means for mom and daughter to communicate when it was just too hard to talk face-to-face. He would give compliments and relay apologies when we humans had trouble finding the right words. He was supposed to continue in our lives and be passed on to her children someday to work his magic with them.

We searched everywhere for him. Made phone calls, put up signs. He just disappeared.

I like to think that Buddy is seeing the sites on his own now. I imagine he's in Southern California, maybe visiting the San Diego Zoo and seeing some real bears, getting some well-deserved rest on the beach. I think we'll start getting postcards from him soon. Who knows? Maybe someday he'll come home again. And boy, will he have some stories to tell us then.

When I first started working at home, I assumed that as my children got older I would have a lot more free time to devote to work. And I do have a little more time, but sometimes I forget that even though my oldest is growing up, she is still a little girl at heart. Whether she's sad about a lost bear or has fears about the future, she still needs her mom. I can't predict those times when she will need me, I just need to be here for her.

I Always Have a Little More to Give

Okay, I admit it. I love chocolate. My kids know if they want to make their Halloween candy last, they need to keep it away from me. One of my greatest joys in life is finding a stray chocolate bar in the Halloween candy bowl after the candy seems to be all picked over. One day last year I went through that bowl with a fine-tooth comb. I had gotten the last of the chocolate out of there. Then that night my daughter shrieked with joy. "Mom! Look what I found!" She triumphantly held a Snickers over her head.

"Where did you get that?" I asked her.

"It was in the Halloween candy."

I couldn't believe it. How could I have missed that? The next day I searched again. If she had found one, maybe there was another one in there. No luck. The chocolate was gone.

Then that night my husband was searching through the candy. "Don't bother," I told him, "the chocolate is all gone."

"No, it isn't," he said, as he pulled another Snickers out of the bowl. "How did you miss this?" he asked.

I wondered too. I usually have chocolate radar. What was happening to me? After a few days of this torture, they confessed. They had a bag of miniature candy bars hidden in the closet, and they planted one in the Halloween candy each night, then waited until I was watching when they magically pulled it out of the bowl—just to torment me.

When I was pregnant with my second daughter, I was a little worried. I loved Nicki so much; I didn't see how another child could possibly measure up. Would I have enough love left over for another child? But then when Dani was born, I realized that I didn't have to cut my love in half, it had been doubled.

Shortly after her little sister was born, Nicki asked me, "Mom, if you had to choose—I know you love us both just the same—but if you *had* to choose one child, which one of us would you choose, me or Dani?"

I think she was looking for reassurance that my love for her hadn't diminished when her little sister was born. I tried to explain it to her, and I'm not sure I did a great job of it.

Many moms worry that they don't have any extra time to run a business in addition to all their other responsibilities. But somehow we manage to find the time for the things that are important.

Now I think I have the perfect analogy. It's like the chocolate in the Halloween candy—we always have a little more to give.

THE LEAST ARE THE GREATEST

I'm reminded of my priorities from time to time. Sometimes my reminders are subtle, and sometimes I have to be hit over the head.

Mike and I teach the high school Sunday school class at our church. We really enjoy the class and the kids; it's one of the highlights of our week. But dealing with one of the boys in class is challenging at times. He has some developmental problems and some- times has trouble doing the work and fitting in with the other kids.

A few weeks ago we were working on a little craft and Bible proj- ect. The students were supposed to find a Bible verse that went along with our project, and this boy was really having a tough time. He has trouble reading and writing, and I could tell he wouldn't be able to do the work. Finally he brought his Bible up to me and asked me to write his verse for him. I was busy, trying to get the other kids their supplies and answer their questions, and I was kind of annoyed that I had to do this for him. But I took his paper, all the while thinking to myself that he shouldn't even be in the class because he can't real- ly keep up, and the other kids can't relate to him, and why am I even teaching this class, I have so many other things to do . . . blah, blah, blah. I'm ashamed of myself now that I look back on it, but that was my reaction.

I told him to at least pick out a verse and I would write it down for him. He opened his Bible and randomly pointed to a verse. I took his Bible and read the verse he was pointing to: "Whoever welcomes this child in my name welcomes me, and whoever welcomes me welcomes the one who sent me; for the least among all of you is the greatest."

I felt as if I had been slapped in the face. This kid was the one who really needed to be "welcomed" and here I was wishing him away. I was in that class for a reason, there's definitely something important there for me to do. But the work I thought was important was trivial, and the least was the greatest.

It's so easy to get caught up in the trivial details of running a business too, trying to cross every *t* and dot every *i*, when the really important things in our lives, the things that really need our time, are starved for our attention.

Be careful, be mindful that you aren't putting too much emphasis on what seems like the "greatest" things, when the "least" might need you most of all. If your kids are trying to get your attention, it's because they need you. They are your greatest; don't make them your least.

DRIVEN TO DISTRACTION

You know how they say dogs can smell your fear? Kids are kind of like that too. They sense our stress, and they're particularly tuned in to our inattention. One day at the grocery store, I was browsing the tabloids while waiting in the checkout line. I started reading an article that contained alleged transcripts of a clandestine meeting between a Hollywood type and someone who was not his wife. My goodness, they really gave the details—word for word. It started to feel a little warm there in the checkout line.

My kids must have noticed I was distracted, because they started asking for everything in sight.

"Mom, can we get some candy?"

"Huh? Sure, whatever."

By the time I came to my senses, we had already checked out. When I unpacked the groceries at home, I realized that my little checkout affair cost me a two-pound bag of M&M's, three packs of gum, and five candy bars. Oh, well, it was worth it.

I hear from moms all the time who write asking how to get marker off their walls or paint out of the carpet. Their e-mails usually start out: "I just left the children alone for five minutes. . . ." I can guess the rest.

If you have young children at home, you will have to do a little more planning and creative scheduling to avoid those unsupervised accidents. Kids can get themselves into trouble so quickly; you really can't risk their safety for the sake of taking a business phone call.

Some moms choose to keep their business completely separate

from their children. They lock their office up in a separate room and don't let anyone in. Others incorporate their business into their family life. I've found that a blend of both approaches works best with my family. While there are times that I must work without any interruptions, there are other times when I welcome my family's input. Nicki designed all my Web site graphics, and Dani suggests ideas for columns and cartoons. I think the fact that they're so involved in the business gives them a feeling of ownership and they're less likely to resent the time I have to spend working. For the most part, though, I work when my kids are at school or sleeping.

Of course, you should consider safety issues when you determine how involved your children can be. If you're making candles, you won't want little ones around the hot wax, but they may be able to help wrap candles or apply labels.

You might also consider arranging for a neighborhood teenager to come to your home some afternoons as a mother's helper, or swap play days with another at-home mom in your area.

Remember, your children will grow up before you know it. You will have many years to work and make money, but you can't get their childhood back. Maybe you won't be able to work full-time until your children are older; maybe you won't become president of a company before you're forty. But you will have the memories of the time you've spent with your children. What could be more important than that? People say it takes a village to raise a child, but I know who's raising mine. I am. That's the most important thing to me.

THEY GROW UP SO FAST

You hear it all the time: "They grow up so fast." I know it's hard to believe when you've been up all night with a crying baby, but take my word for it, they really do grow up fast. It seems like it was just last weekend when my oldest daughter was born. Then I turned around and I was sending her off to kindergarten.

I'll never forget that first day of kindergarten, standing there with all the other parents as our kids lined up for their first day of school. Some parents were crying, some were thrilled, I was nervous. We parents were instructed to write our child's name on his or her name tag and below that write how our child would get home from school that day. I wrote out Nicki's name tag, and the children lined up. I noticed her classmates' name tags:

REBECCA
MOM

JILL
BUS

Then my daughter's:

Nicole (Nicki) Demas
My mom (Cheryl Demas)
will drive me home
in our family car.
She will pick me up
in the south parking lot
after school.

I almost needed two name tags to fit it all in. Once I realized what I had done, I was worried. My poor daughter. Would the other children make fun of her? Was it too late to change her tag? I started out in search of another blank name tag, and my husband had to drag me away. "Just let her go, Cheryl."

I have the same problem—getting too caught up with the

details—in my business life too. Sometimes I just have to step back to see the big picture and not get bogged down in trivia. If you have this problem too, consider holding weekly or monthly meetings with another work-at-home mom or people in your family who support your business—a kind of informal board of directors. Run your business plans past them. Let them help you see the big picture, and let them help you see when you just need to "let it go."

Now all of a sudden my daughter is old enough to drive, and I'm still nervous. I know it won't be much longer and she'll be off to college. I find I'm telling myself almost every day now, "Just let her go, Cheryl."

But it just went by so fast.

I got a clue that my daughter is growing up when we attended an ice show recently. She yawned through the costumed characters and parade of animals. They didn't catch her attention. What really made her sit up and take notice was when Tarzan skated out onto the ice in his tiny little loincloth. That's my girl.

Another clue that my daughter is growing up is that we're suddenly getting service at the mall. Sales boys used to wait on me, but not anymore. I will be standing, searching for someone to serve me at the music store for twenty minutes. Then my daughter walks in and four sales "boys" appear out of thin air. At the deli we get extra cookies in our bag, our beverages are supersize—no charge. At restaurants her glass is never empty. The waiter checks back so often, just to "see how we're doing," we couldn't possibly run out of anything. So this is service. Now I know why we never got service before. All the waiters were waiting on the teenage girls.

I know how much I appreciate personal attention from a business—when I can get it—so I try to be aware of this in my business too. Each customer, large or small, young or old, deserves to be treated equally.

Having my girls seven and half years apart has been a blessing in so many ways. I would never have planned to have such a large gap between children, but now I realize the benefits.

When Nicki was little, I was always looking ahead to the next milestone. I tracked her progress in baby books and growth charts, always anticipating what she would be doing next. Rolling over, sitting up, crawling, walking. Now that I have the perspective of how quickly she grew up, I'm not nearly as anxious to push my little girl along. I'm happy to give her time to grow at her own pace.

But now I *know* what I have to look forward to. Once Dani hits her teenage years, I'll be able to get real service again.

New Year's Resolutions

Several years ago as we were preparing for New Year's, I listed my resolutions. They were my usual resolutions: lose weight, exercise, save money. The same list I always write. I asked my little girl if she had a New Year's resolution. She seemed confused, so I told her, "Think about the one thing you would like to be able to do this year. For example, you might have a goal of learning to write your ABCs. Tell me anything you can think of that you want to do this year."

She thought for a while longer and finally said, "This year, I would like to . . . eat more candy!"

Now, the more I think about it, I believe we get enough of the "plan your work and work your plan" type of advice. We all know that we need to work, and work hard, if we want to be successful. What we need to hear more is "enjoy the journey." I may never reach that skinny, wealthy "paradise" of my dreams, but I can learn to enjoy each step of the way.

Every year after that candy incident, I've resolved to take life a lit-

THIS YEAR I RESOLVE TO:

1. LOSE 50 POUNDS
2. MAKE A MILLION DOLLARS
3. BE PATIENT AND CHEERFUL AT ALL TIMES
4. SET REALISTIC GOALS

tle less seriously. I'll resolve to tell more jokes and splash in the tub more, and not just at New Year's, but every day. My daughter's second-grade class had career day recently, and Dani has decided that she wants to be a screenwriter when she grows up. She says she will write only comedies though, "because we need more laughs in the world." I couldn't agree more, Dani; laugh it up. It makes us all happier, and I'm sure our dentist appreciates it too.

It's a Beautiful Day!

When my first daughter was born, I was committed to filling her life with only positive influences. I vowed to greet her with a cheery "It's a beautiful day" as I picked her up out of her crib each morning. I really was happy too. There's nothing like a baby to make you look forward to each day. They wake up with so much anticipation and enthusiasm. . . . I couldn't help but really believe that it was a beautiful day with her.

Then she became a toddler and started talking. And some mornings I was a little more drowsy and not quite as quick getting in there to get her out of bed. If I wasn't Johnny-on-the-spot, she would call out, "Mom, it's a beautiful day." And if she still didn't get a response, she would say a little louder, "Mom! It's a beautiful day!" Until eventually she would be standing in her crib screaming, "MOM! IT'S A BEAUTIFUL DAY!" The phrase loses some of its cheery optimism when screamed.

So for her, "It's a beautiful day" came to mean, "Get in here and get me out of this crib, *right now*!"

What we say isn't always what we mean in our house. For example, when my oldest daughter was little I was making tuna fish salad, and she saw me put in the Miracle Whip and asked what I was doing. I said, "making tuna fish." So, in her mind, Miracle Whip was tuna fish.

A few days later, I was working and my husband was watching the kids. I asked him to please take care of them, I really didn't want to be disturbed.

He was making bologna sandwiches for lunch. (Do you get the impression we're not health food nuts?) Thinking back to the Miracle Whip, our daughter asked him to put tuna fish on her bologna sandwich. Not wanting to make waves, he did as she asked. Of course, she freaked out when he served her the strange concoction.

I came in to see what was causing all the commotion, which was what he was trying to avoid in the first place. Imagine my surprise to see my frustrated husband, my screaming daughter, and a bologna-and-tuna-fish sandwich on the table.

When Dani was in preschool, I realized how careful I have to be when I communicate with her too. She came home from school one day and asked me, "Mom, will I ever have to stay home with a beaver?"

We had raccoons out on our back deck once, but that's the only wildlife we've ever seen near our home, so this question kind of threw me. "No, Dani, I can't ever imagine that happening. Why do you ask?"

"Our teacher said that Robbie wouldn't be at school today because he is home with a beaver," she explained.

Then it dawned on me. "Oh, a fever. Robbie is home with a fever." That was a relief, but it made me realize that I probably say a lot of things that confuse her. One day I told her that a piece of pizza had "her name on it." She looked and looked and finally said, "I just don't see it, Mom."

"See what?"

"My name—on the pizza."

Dealing with these miscommunications has taught me that I need to be careful in my business communication too. Customers and clients can misunderstand what I'm saying just as easily as my family. E-mail is notorious for causing communication problems. Humor and especially sarcasm can be easily misinterpreted, so be especially careful when typing e-mail. Don't assume that your business associates are hearing what you think you're saying. Also restate what you hear from your associates and verify that you are talking about the same thing. Then get it in writing. It's so much easier to do the communication work up-front than to try to repair miscommunication after the damage has been done.

We almost had a communication disaster at home when Dani was still in diapers and it was Dad's turn at diaper duty. She told him, "Dad, put ice cream on my butt." At first he thought that maybe I had started some kind of natural diaper rash treatment.

"Is that what Mom does?" he asked her.

She assured him that I always used ice cream when I changed her diaper. But he thought back to the tuna fish incident and this seemed just a little too strange. He asked her to clarify and show him where

Mom keeps the ice cream. She grabbed the tube of diaper rash cream. What a relief.

Thank goodness he's learned not to take every request literally.

MY TOUGH CUSTOMER

I've been dealing with a particularly difficult customer lately. Have you ever had a customer whom you wanted to please so much, yet whatever you did, it never seemed to be enough? It seems that no matter what I do, I can never make her happy.

I do more for her than I've ever done for anyone else, and she does show glimmers of appreciation. Yet lately, nothing I do seems to be good enough. The other night I ran into her at a social gathering and she walked right by me! It was as if I didn't exist. She spent the

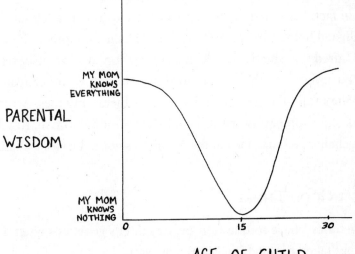

night avoiding me, pretending she didn't even know me. She acts as if she doesn't want to be seen in my presence.

When she comes to me with a problem, I give her my opinion on the best course of action. Then what does she do? Exactly the opposite of what I've told her, with the expected disastrous results. And then she has the nerve to come to me, cry on my shoulder, and ask me to pick up the pieces.

But I consider my work with this customer to be *the* most important job I have ever done, so I'm willing to put up with the frustrations. I need to see this project through, and I'm determined that we can work together to reach a successful conclusion.

Would you work with such a customer? No? Well, if you have young children, get ready, your tough customer is right around the corner, and he or she will be knocking on your door sooner than you think.

My tough customer? My teenage daughter.

In fact, her fantasy is that one of these days her father and I will finally tell her the truth. We'll tell her that she's adopted. Then she'll be assured that she has no genetic connection to us whatsoever.

But even with the ups and downs, working with her really is a joy. She's full of surprises, and she keeps me on my toes. Actually, I think she is preparing me to be a better businesswoman. Any business challenge I may face in the future has got to be easier than this.

It's a Good Thing

Sometimes I have to question my daughter's genetics myself. Lately she has taken to watching Martha Stewart.

One day at the grocery store, Nicki picked up a little vegetable brush and said, "Mom, do you know what this is good for?"

"Well, cleaning vegetables I suppose."

"Yes, of course. But it also helps you iron fringe."

"Iron fringe?"

"Yes. You see, you use this brush to straighten and untangle the fringe and then you apply your iron with just a little bit of steam, and voilà! Our fringe is straight and neat again."

"Voilà? Fringe? What fringe? What are you talking about?"

My iron doesn't exactly get a workout and it certainly has never touched fringe. I don't even think we own anything with fringe. She shrugged her shoulders and we proceeded to the produce department. "Oh, Mom, I know of a delightful recipe for apples. Isn't this just the best time of year for apples?"

"Well, sure, I guess so. It's fall and all."

"Yes, as I was saying, I know of a great recipe for baked apples.

THE DANGER WITH RAISING
ENTREPRENEURIAL CHILDREN

The thing that makes them truly wonderful is the addition of just a dollop of delightful cream sauce served on the side when you plate the apples."

"Plate the apples? Iron my fringe? Nicki, what has gotten into you?"

Her next words shocked me: "Well, I didn't want to tell you. I've been watching Martha Stewart, Mom. You should watch too. She really does have great ideas."

Where did I go wrong? I wouldn't even buy Nicki a toy vacuum cleaner when she was little because I didn't want her to get the impression that domestic work would be her lot in life. Now she's watching Martha Stewart?

While other moms are worrying about the influence of MTV and rock videos on their children, I've got Martha Stewart influencing mine.

Kids just have to rebel, don't they?

She wasn't always this way. She used to admire us. She used to be proud of me. I thought I saw a flash of the old her the other day when we were ice-skating together. I usually let my daughters skate alone and use the time to have some coffee and relax or catch up on some paperwork. But this time I decided to rent a pair of skates for myself. Much to my daughters' amazement, I slowly skated onto the ice. Of course, I knew that I wasn't in the running for the U.S. Olympic team, but I thought I was doing pretty well. At least I hadn't fallen—yet. I waved to my teenage daughter; I could tell she was trying to tell me something, but I couldn't quite hear her. I skated closer.

"What?" I yelled to her.

It sounded like she was saying: "Mom! Be careful you don't fall."

How sweet, she was worried about my safety. How many teenagers would be so concerned about their mom? I skated closer to hear her better. This time I heard her loud and clear.

"Mom! You look like a great big goofball!"

There's no danger of getting an inflated ego with a teenager in the house. The other day, I was feeling pretty good about myself. I had this new book to work on, I had gotten some positive feedback on my Web site. Then I had to push my luck.

"Nicki? What's it like having such a cool mom?"

"Mom," she shot back, "you're not cool." And then just to make sure I was completely deflated, she added, "and you're not funny."

Yes, she keeps my ego in check. And that's a good thing.

MOTHER-DAUGHTER COMMUNICATION

It used to be so difficult to communicate with my oldest daughter. She was always out and about, coming and going to school and activities. We could barely keep track of her. So we got her a cell phone to ease our communication problems. It used to be difficult to talk to her . . . now it's impossible.

I can't reach my daughter on her cell phone, but I can reach all her friends.

"Hello."

"Hello, Nicki?"

"No, this is Molly."

"I'm sorry. I must have called the wrong number."

"No, this is Nicole's phone. I'm just borrowing it to call my mom."

"Do you know where Nicole is?"

"No, I got her phone from Tiff. She got it from Laura, who got it from Sam."

"I thought Sam had her own phone."

"Oh, yeah, she does. But Nicole was using it. Um, I need to make my call now, okay?"

On the other hand, my little girl is *always* talking to me. Although she has never spoken a single word to me without first reciting:

"Mom . . . Mom . . . Mom . . . Mom . . . until I say, "Yes?"

"Do you know what?"

And then she waits for me to say, "What?"

After all that (if she's remembered what she first came to tell me), she begins her story.

I love it that she so willingly shares her thoughts with me, and I occasionally have to remind myself that whatever she's telling me is important to her. Sometimes I get so wrapped up in my work, trying to get everything done at once, that I need to stop what I'm doing and really listen. I know it won't be long before I descend from the mountain of "My mom knows everything" into the valley of "My mom is driving me crazy!" I know these days will pass all too quickly, and I'll be wishing I could hear "Mom . . . Mom . . . Mom . . . Mom" again.

I'm not too old to remember the things my own mom said that drove me crazy. I remember the way she would wait up for me at night. When she finally heard the door open, she would call out from her bedroom, "Is that you?"

"Yeah, Mom, I'm home."

It drove me crazy. Can you name one person in the world who could answer no to that question? "Is that you?" Who else could it be?

Now, though, I think back on those days and I can identify with my mother. In fact, sometimes I think I'm channeling her. Her words come out of my mouth before I even realize what I'm saying.

The mother of a dear friend of mine passed away unexpectedly. When I called my friend, she was going over and over her last conversation with her mother.

"I'm pretty sure I said 'I love you' when I said good-bye, but I'm not sure," she said.

She so wanted to know that those were the last words that had passed between them.

But as mothers we know that we say "I love you" in many ways, from "Be careful" to "What do you see in him?" and, yes, even in "Is that you?" I'm sure their last words to each other were "I love you," spoken or not.

And what I would give now to hear my mom call out, "Is that you?" when I walk in the front door of my home. In fact, my vision of heaven is that when I open those pearly gates, I'll hear my mom call out . . .

"Is that you?"

And I'll say, "Yeah, Mom, I'm home."

One last time.

CAN WE EAT AT THE NEIGHBOR'S HOUSE?

We try to eat together as a family as often as possible. We all agree that this is important, and I realize it's not all that common anymore. One night when we sat down to dinner, one of my daughter's friends said, "Is it Thanksgiving or something? Why is everyone sitting down to eat at the same time?"

But my daughters turn up their noses at any food I serve them that doesn't come with a toy or have a cartoon character on the box. It's so frustrating. I imagine I've come up with something they'll like, buy all the ingredients, cook a special dinner, and then they won't even taste it.

If they tasted it and then rejected it, I could take that as a critique of my cooking. But they won't even taste anything new—that is, at our house. Send them to a neighbor's or a friend's house and they're as adventurous as Julia Child.

The other day my neighbor said she was grilling seafood and invited the girls over for dinner. I kind of smirked and said, "Sure, but I doubt if they'll eat much more than some bread. They aren't very adventurous when it comes to food."

"Well," she smirked back at me, "we'll see."

Later, when the girls got home, they started to tell me about their dinner, but I interrupted: "Right, I know what was served, but tell me, what did you actually eat?"

"Well, we started with salmon-stuffed tomatoes, followed by grilled tuna. It was so good!" They raved on and on.

Another time my little girl came home and told me, "Mom! We had the best dinner. You should make it sometime. It's called steak!"

I guess it's the old "the grass is always greener" story. For some reason, nothing homegrown seems as intriguing or wonderful as what's happening or served somewhere else.

Are you doing this with your home business too? Do you look at other work-at-home moms and think, "I wish my business were like

that"? Does it seem like everyone else is doing great things? Do you look at other sites and businesses with envy?

I've talked to a lot of moms, and they all have different ways of running their businesses. Remember that your business reflects you and your personality. You really wouldn't want it to be like someone else's, would you? How boring that would be, if we were all alike. Take pride in your uniqueness, your special style and way of doing things. You will find a way to be successful, and you can be proud that you did it in your own way.

It might be tuna casserole instead of grilled tuna steaks, but one is not necessarily better than the other. The important thing is, it's your tuna casserole, and that alone makes it special.

Bookstores and Alligators

We had spent a little too long at the bookstore the other day, and I was trying to hurry my daughter out the door. If you knew my kids, you would know that they don't do anything quickly. She was slowly making her way toward the exit, jumping from white tile to white tile, carefully avoiding the blue (water) tiles.

As I waited for her by the door, a greeting card caught my eye. It said, "I don't take my problems to work, I leave them at child care."

Maybe that was supposed to be a joke, but it made me sad to think that parents would ever describe their kids as problems. I was brought back to "reality" when my daughter shouted, "Look out, Mom! You almost stepped on an alligator!"

The tiles had apparently transformed themselves into alligator-infested swampland.

I guess this might seem like a problem to some people, a little girl

who won't move quickly, a mom in a hurry. But really, what could be more important in my life right now? What could need my attention more than this little girl who has placed herself in the middle of an alligator swamp?

So we hopped and skipped out the door, drawing some strange looks I'm sure. Strange looks from those who don't know about alligator swamps in the bookstore or, perhaps more likely, from those who have long since forgotten about them.

Do you ever find yourself saying, "Well, someday when I have more time I can play with my kids more"? or "Someday when we have more money in the bank, I will be able to spend more time with my family"?

There are times, when a loved one is lost through accident or illness, that we are reminded just how fragile our lives can be. We see someone whose life is cut short, and we remember that life isn't always fair or predictable.

So be careful that you aren't putting off the really important things in your life, creating problems where there really aren't any . . . and always waiting for someday. . . .

Because sometimes, someday doesn't come.

I'm Alone in Here

When my daughter was twelve, she attended a sleepover where one of the girls brought R-rated videos. Nicki knew the videos would give her nightmares, yet she was torn between wanting to come home and staying. She knew if she left, she'd be labeled a dweeb. But if she stayed, she wouldn't enjoy herself. She didn't want to feel pressured into doing something she didn't want to do or watching a movie she didn't want to see. At 1:00 A.M. my phone rang.

"Mom, I want to come home," she whispered, "but I don't want my friends to be mad at me."

"This is a perfect opportunity to blame your exit on good old Mom," I said. "Just say what I tell you to say, and you'll have a way out."

"Nicki," I continued, "you must come home right now!" Then I whispered, "Now you say, 'But, Mom! I don't want to leave.'"

Nicki protested, "Mom, what are you doing?"

"Just trust me, Nicki. Do as I say and you'll have an excuse to leave without looking like a dweeb."

"But, Mom."

"Just say it, Nicki!"

"Okay," she agreed. "But, Mom," she said weakly, "I don't want to leave."

"You come home right now young lady, I will not allow you to watch that movie!"

"Now you say, 'Come home? Now? But Mom, I want to watch it; let me stay, please!'"

"But, Mom," she said again.

"Nicki," I interrupted her, "just repeat what I tell you; why won't you cooperate?"

"Because, Mom"—finally I had stopped talking long enough to listen—"I'm alone in here."

Do you ever feel alone in here? Working at home, alone, can be isolating. But it doesn't have to be that way. Not only that, you can't *let* it be that way. No matter what your situation—work-at-home mom, stay-at-home mom, working mom . . . you need to continue to make new contacts, meet new friends, new people all the time.

Harvey Mackay says, "If you want one year of prosperity, grow grain. If you want ten years of prosperity, grow trees. If you want one hundred years of prosperity, grow people."

If you want to grow your business and expand your opportunities, expand your own horizons, you need to get out—physically get out and meet new people, or if you live in a rural area, through the Internet. Challenge yourself to break out of your comfort zone. You may need to go little by little at first. Introduce yourself to a new parent at school, join a club, and sign up for a class with your children. If you think about it, you'll find many ways to meet new people and stay in touch with old friends: through your child's school, at the grocery store, via e-mail or mailing lists. You never know when you'll make a great new business contact or start a new friendship.

My daughter did decide to come home from the sleepover that night, all on her own. She may have been alone in there while she made her call home, but her good friends were there for her, and they understood. You don't have to feel "alone in here" anymore either. Get out and meet people today.

REMEMBER THEIR "LASTS"

We mothers tend to pay a lot of attention to firsts. First steps, first words, first day of school. You may be working at home because you don't want to miss out on any of those important firsts.

But don't forget about the "lasts." We can't be as aware of the lasts in our children's lives, because we usually don't realize they've occurred until much later. But the memories can be just as precious.

Some lasts are easy to remember. Like the last time I carried my sleeping daughter in from the car. My back decided that would be the last time I'd do that. But when was the last time my teenager wanted to snuggle in my lap to watch a movie? Or hold my hand to cross the street?

The other evening, my little girl ran into the house, out of breath. "Mom, you've to see this! Hurry up!" she told me.

I ran out into the driveway just as my neighbor was coming out of her house too. Both girls had run inside to fetch their moms. Such

DID YOU BUY
TICKETS FOR
THIS MOM ?

NO IT'S FREE

I'M AMAZED THAT
THEY CAN DO THIS
FOR NO CHARGE
EVERY SINGLE NIGHT!

excitement is usually reserved for the ice-cream man, but there was no ice-cream man in sight. "What caused all this excitement?" we wondered.

"Look!" they both said, pointing to the sky, "Isn't it beautiful?"

We looked up to see—the sunset, and yes, it was beautiful. However, not something I would normally run out of the house to see.

It made me think that there probably wouldn't be too many more times that my daughter would run into the house in her excited little-girl way. But just as the sunset signaled the end of the day and held the promise of a new sunrise and a new tomorrow, my children's "lasts" hold the promise for a lot of new "firsts" for them too. I'm glad I'm here for the firsts in my daughters' lives, and lately I've been thankful for the lasts too. I've decided to pay a little more attention to the simple moments. I know now that this won't last forever, but I want to hold on to the memories.

"Wow, Jordyn was right," my daughter said as we turned around to go back into the house.

"Right about what?" I asked her.

"Sunsets don't last very long."

"No, they don't," I thought, "but their memories do."

SURVIVAL TIPS FROM SISTER ZOOS
Working and Children

I compare being a work-from-home mom to watching a good ballet performance—it looks a lot easier than it is! I bought my current home to turn it into a B&B. My son Noah had just turned three. Three is such a charming age; my guests loved him. What a perfect little host. He'd bring in the basket of breads in the morning and the guests would love it. Little did they know he was just angling for a fresh muffin.

Then enter Carson two years later! Carson had colic for three months, and we would race to take him to the other end of the house so as not to wake the guests. But we soon found that our guests loved having a baby in the house. More than once I'd find him rocking on the porch in some grandma-type's lap after leaving him with my husband. I'd feel guilty . . . perhaps they thought my husband wasn't doing a good job and they were babysitting. But it turned out that they just missed their own grandbaby and were enjoying a snuggle with my little guy. If they did hear a cry in the night, their sympathies were with me at having to get up so early to make breakfast.

What I've learned from this is that any person who has ever had a child fully realizes how hard it is. And—much to my amazement—will do whatever is possible to help out! Working from home is not for everyone, but as parents who put off children until later in life, we wanted to be the major influence in our children's lives. We've made financial and ego sacrifices. And it has been worth it. We continue to enjoy the ride.

Karen E., North Carolina, River-House.com

I don't even bother trying to work when my kids are home. It's next to impossible to get anything productive done while they are here and awake, so I just check e-mail periodically during the day and do the bulk of my work at night after they have gone to bed. I try to be Mom and keep in mind why I started this home business in the first place—because I wanted to be home with my children.

Amanda F., Wisconsin, FamilyCorner.com

I feel it's very important to project a professional image of my business, so I can't have children making noise in the background. Of course, my children are involved in my business; they've tested products and helped with reviews. But I've kept a clear line between business and family.

Having a mom who runs her own businesses has been an excellent example for my children. Now they think that running a business is the most natural thing in the world. They each have their own businesses already. They even ask their grandma, "So, what businesses did you run when you were younger, Grandma?"

Elizabeth, K., California, Homeschool.com

When my kids were younger, they loved my business—after all, I am the "Toy Lady"! I was one of the most popular at career day at school. Twice each year it's like Christmas when I get my shipment of new toys . . . and they were my toy testers. Then they became teenagers! My daughter, who is my oldest and who always wanted to be a toy lady when she grew up, suddenly was a little embarrassed. "Mom, do you *have* to talk to every person with a baby?"

But now she's in college, thinking more seriously about what she wants to be when she grows up. She's told me several times how much it has meant for me to be home and there for her after school, just to talk. And whatever she ends up doing, she wants it to be something flexible around someday having children. Who knows, she may be a toy lady yet.

And the new toys still come every six months, and I love to see my son, now six feet three inches, down on the floor, still testing them all out.

Nancy J., Texas

My husband stays home full-time with our children while I work in my home office. This is a great solution for us; my husband is a better mom than I am!

Since I deal with large companies, I have to maintain a professional image with my customers. When my son does happen to wander into my office and make noise when I'm on the phone with a customer, I apologize for the noise and explain that my office is next-door to the corporate day-care center.

Debra L., Pennsylvania, YourSafeChild.com

My sons had their second- and third-grade open house at the beginning of the school year, and my husband couldn't attend, so my sons and I went up to the school, with their one-and-one-half-year-old toddler sister, to visit their classroom and the teachers. The first place my daughter headed was for the classroom computer! She pulled out the little chair, plopped down, and put her little hands up to the keyboard. I'm sure she was imitating Mom, and luckily the teachers laughed and told her to keep it up!

Brenda H., Michigan, OldFashionedLiving.com

My children like helping with my stamping business so much that I have to leave some of the work until they're in bed. I occasionally have to work with a particular very messy ink, and I know they just couldn't resist helping Mom "work" if they were around when I used it, so I do that work only when they're sleeping. Other than that, I appreciate their help.

Melissa O., Massachusetts, StampFolk.com

PROBLEM

I can't keep my kids quiet when I'm on a business phone call.

SOLUTIONS FROM SISTER ZOOS

This used to be a huge problem for me too. My suggestion is to get an answering service. Not an answering machine, because people won't leave a message sometimes and that's not good for business, but an answering service with a real person taking the message, and then you can call back when the kids are quiet, napping, or at school.

Kylie A., New South Wales, Australia

Duct tape. . . . Really, though, schedule calls for nap times or times when the kids are entertained or playing. Get a cordless phone so you can get away from the noise—if possible. If another caregiver is home, sit in your car if you need silence on the phone.

Nancy P., California

Make your business calls as short as possible. Don't schedule too many at the same time. Take time to sit and talk to your kids after the calls to give them attention. Make sure they know that you need this time of quiet but that you will spend time with them right afterward. You can also use a kitchen timer and let them know that when it goes off, you will get off the phone and spend time with them.

Alanna W., Oklahoma

After several frustrating months of dealing with this problem, I've found the best thing to do is not answer the phone when my son is present or awake. He attends day care three hours a day, so from 8:30 to 11:30, there's no problem. When he's home I let my answering service pick up, and then I return calls when he takes his afternoon nap or the next morning when he's gone. Even when I'm on a personal call, he cuts up so badly sometimes that I don't answer the phone after "business hours" either. It can be really frustrating, but I guess he just wants my attention.

Myra T., Louisiana

Snack time was made for phone time!

Calissa L., Florida

Have a play area set up to entertain them while you are on the phone and put in a movie while you are on calls. There are also plenty of educational programs that you can buy or check out from your local library to take home and entertain the children while you're working on the phone.

Diann S., New Hampshire

The phone problem is a big one at our house. My kids now behave better than my husband does while I am on a phone call if I cannot find a quiet place to talk. (Sometimes the bathroom works great for this!) I have some special markers and paper locked in my desk. I keep stickers in there also. When an important call is being made, I will ask the person to hold for ten seconds and get the supplies out for the kids. I am a mother of five, and all my kids look forward to being able to make some pictures with the "special" supplies.

Amy S., Wisconsin

I handle phone calls several ways: I try to make and take business calls while the children are at school or when there is another adult around to help keep them quiet. If I don't have those luxuries, I take the time to tell my children that I am making a business phone call or picking up a business call and that I need them to be quiet so that I may talk. If I am still interrupted, I give a stern face and point for them to go to another room. If that doesn't work, I politely ask the caller to hold so that I can correct the problem or find out what the emergency is.

Roberta S., Florida

I explain to my kids (they are three and five) that Mommy has to make an important call for work. Depending on how serious it is, I will either put in a short movie or turn on a PBS show or set them up with a computer game. I always close the door to my office and hang a SSSHHHH sign that I made, so they remember before they bang on the door or come running in that I am on the phone. They have come in a couple of times, but I make the "shhh" sign with my finger and they know to be quiet. Most of the time all they need is a hug or to know where I'm at. None of my clients know I work from home.

April G., Washington

Though the media will have us believe that our child will sit quietly while we conduct crucial business, that image couldn't be further from the truth. Invariably this is the exact moment when they'll discover a new, extensive repertoire of ear-piercing sounds.

To avoid this trap, I communicate as often as possible via e-mail. It doesn't matter if my son is blowing raspberries while I type—and I've actually found that people respond more often and more promptly to e-mail correspondence than to phone messages.

Mikalee D., Nevada

So you've taken care of your business, your home, your husband, your children, that about covers everything, doesn't it? Oh, yeah, there's one more thing that needs to be taken care of . . . *you!*

11

The Zookeeper

Taking Care of Yourself
(As Well As Your Home, Your Kids, Your
Husband, and Your Business)

THE HIPPO ENCLOSURE

As we continue our tour through the zoo that is my life, we approach the hippo exhibit. It didn't start out this way. This used to be the home of the svelte gazelle. Then she started spending ten to twelve hours a day sitting on her butt in front of a computer.

I've gained and lost and gained again . . . probably about fifty pounds since I started working at home. I'm somewhere in the middle now. I used to be able to use the "but I just had a baby" excuse, but I think I have to stop using that by the time my "baby" gets her driver's license.

As you know, we moms say good-bye to any sense of privacy as soon as we have children. I realized this as I was lying in a stark room with my legs spread apart and a small crowd peering between them—and that was just the conception! The delivery room is another story altogether.

My bathroom has also become a public place. So when I was taking a shower one day, I wasn't surprised when my little girl threw back the shower curtain and peeked in. "Hey, Dad?" she said. Now, that surprised me, and it's very bad news for:

A. Me, because naked, I look like my husband.

B. My husband, because naked, I look like him.

C. My daughter, for not being able to tell the difference.

The correct answer is probably "all of the above."

Working at home and spending a lot of time on the computer obviously haven't done much for my fitness or shape. So in an effort to end shower-time identity mix-ups, I have tried a variety of different diet and exercise programs.

My husband has tried his own variety of programs, the most recent being a sandwich-shop plan he saw on TV. He eats a sub sandwich for lunch and dinner and that's it. For weeks that was all I heard about. WWJD came to mean "What would Jared do?" in our house. Until one day when I called Mike on his cell phone. When he answered, I heard, "Would you like fries with that?" in the background.

"What was that?" I asked. "Where are you?"

"Um, just getting some lunch." He answered.

"At a drive-through?"

"Yes, at a drive-through."

"You can't get a sub at a drive-through. And fries? You're getting fries?"

SO... YOU RESOLVED TO *GAIN* WEIGHT THIS YEAR?

WHEN SCALES ATTACK

"Well, I just had a craving, it's not like I do it every day."

"Oh, you are *so* busted!" I told him. Never again would I listen to his bragging about his diet. What were the odds that I would happen to call him just as he was in the drive-through? It had to be fate.

Mike has other dubious dieting theories. He claims that by continuously cutting something in half it will never be completely eaten. Since he always eats just half, in theory he never eats the whole thing and thus saves calories. And that last microscopic piece of food always ends up back in the refrigerator. We have slivers of chocolate cake that were around in the last millennium. I actually have several long-term residents in my kitchen appliances. It's just easier that way. If a bowl comes out of the dishwasher not completely clean, I give it another chance and run it through with the next load. I have one bowl that's been in there for three years.

Now I'm thinking that what I need to do is find a good exercise video. Oh, I already own several videos, dating back to the classic Jane Fonda laser disc. Turns out, one has to actually do the exercises along with the video; it's not enough just to watch it. Either that's my problem, or I just haven't found the right video yet.

So it was with this in mind that I went to the video store. As I was browsing through the workout section, a young man approached me.

"Have you ever heard of this?" he asked, as he held up a yoga video.

"Yoga? Sure." I replied.

His next question surprised me.

"Have you ever done it naked?"

Now, I hadn't expected *that*. I just shook my head in stunned silence. Did I look like a naked-yoga practitioner to him? How would you like to be in that class at your local health club? I don't even like to *shower* naked at the club; at least let me keep my clothes on while I exercise.

I know just the people who would do it too. I see them strutting around the locker room, obviously proud of the results of their workout routines. I'd rather not see my neighbors and the school principal in their birthday suits, and vice versa. It's a classic catch-22, I don't want to work out until I get in shape, and I won't get in shape until I work out.

So for now I'll stay safely tucked away, exercising in the privacy of my own home . . . and if I do give the naked yoga a try, I'll make sure the blinds are closed.

INTERNATIONAL TRADE

WAHMs are busy ladies, but don't let that be an excuse for not taking care of yourself. Running a home business can take its toll on a

I'VE DECIDED TO COMBINE THE HIGH-PROTEIN DIET *AND* THE HIGH-CARBOHYDRATE DIET... I FIGURE I'LL LOSE WEIGHT TWICE AS FAST!

mom. Be careful that you don't run yourself into the ground while you're running your business and taking care of your family. Supermom is a fictional character. Turn off those voices in your head that tell you what you "should" do. You know better than anyone else what is best for you and your family. Listen to your heart and take care of the most important things.

From time to time I get other reminders that a good workout routine is called for. Believe it or not, there was a time when one couldn't buy Pokemon merchandise here in the United States. But my daughters had caught Pokemon fever, and when they learned that I had a connection in Japan, they came up with a plan.

"Mom, find out if you can buy something here that your friend in Japan would want. Then you can send it to her in exchange for Pokemon stuff for us," they told me.

Well, it wasn't a bad idea, so I asked my friend in Japan what she thought of it. Was there anything in the United States that she would be willing to exchange for Pokemon merchandise?

"As a matter of fact, there is. Furbies are very popular here, but we can't buy them anywhere. Can you get a couple Furbies?" she asked.

Could I get Furbies? Does Oprah like sweet potato pie? Of course I could get Furbies. So I told her to get me those Pokemons and we'd have a deal.

Now, this was during the height of Furby mania here too, so they weren't really that easy to get. But I knew I could do it. Our newspaper had an ad from the toy store at the mall. They had a limited number of Furbies that would be sold to the first customers at the store on Friday morning, the Friday after Thanksgiving, at 6:00 A.M. I don't usually brave the crowds at the mall on the day after Thanksgiving, and I'd never been to the mall at 6:00 A.M. in my life. But for the sake of international relations, I was willing to give it a try.

I got up that morning at 4:00 and was at the mall before 5:00. I knew I would have to be there well in advance of opening time, as I expected that there would be a big crowd. I brought a book to read while I waited and a cup of coffee.

When I arrived, I discovered that the veteran shoppers already had a system in place. There were those who obviously knew what they were doing and had already staked out their positions in front of the doors. Even in the pouring rain, the atmosphere was festive. The veterans had all the details; There were one hundred Furbies, the limit was two per person. They graciously shared tips with us "first timers." We had a lot of fun swapping shopping stories. I didn't even need my book to pass the time. Yes, there was a great feeling of cama-raderie . . . until the doors opened.

At precisely 5:30 A.M., mall security unlocked the first of the out-side doors. Then it was just like in the movies. Any sense of community evaporated and it was every man, woman, and child for him- or herself. Those who were "lucky" enough to be near the first unlocked doors were swept into the mall ahead of the others. "But wait," I wanted to shout, "shouldn't we line up and proceed in an orderly fashion? Following the order in which we first arrived here at the mall?" There was no avoiding being pulled along with the crowd, and soon hundreds of us were sprinting toward the toy store.

Playing on the mall's sound system was the theme from *Chariots of Fire,* which either was a bizarre coincidence or someone at the mall had a twisted sense of humor. So there we were, hundreds of shoppers—moms, grandmas and grandpas, dads and children—all running through the mall at 5:30 A.M. to the theme from *Chariots of Fire.*

Although I may appear to be a natural athlete, remember, I am actually quite slow. Even slower while running with my nonfat latte, and with my raincoat flapping behind me. I made a quick mental calculation: one hundred Furbies, two per person; I had to be in that first fifty. I knew I couldn't be at the front of the line, but I was lucky enough to have been pretty close to the doors when they opened. It looked like I was going to make it. I'd just glance over my shoulder and . . . oh no! Grandma and Grandpa were running too, and they were gaining on me!

As I rounded the corner and passed the Gap, two things became painfully clear: (1) I really need to get more exercise, and (2) I'd *really* hate to have a heart attack while running for a Furby at the mall.

I managed to make it to the toy store fast enough to get the Furbies, and I'm happy to say that Grandma and Grandpa got their Furbies too. I don't know if I could have lived with the guilt if they hadn't.

My daughters got their Pokemon merchandise, our Furbies are living it up in Japan, and I'm still out of shape. But I'll give Grandma and Grandpa a run for their money next year.

A Gift for You

Do you realize how much candy is a part of almost every holiday? There are candy canes at Christmas, chocolate on Valentine's Day, candy eggs at Easter, but the mother of all the candy holidays is Halloween. I dreaded that first Halloween after my daughter was diagnosed with diabetes. I was afraid that one of her favorite holidays would become just another occasion for sadness, or a reminder of everything she couldn't have.

So that first postdiagnosis Halloween, we made an arrangement. I agreed to buy all her trick-or-treating candy at the rate of ten cents per piece. Nicki had always enjoyed trick-or-treating, but she was never willing to stay out for too long. I thought I was pretty safe with my ten-cent deal.

Because of bad weather, there weren't many trick-or-treaters out that year; everyone had extra candy. She made sure everyone knew about our arrangement, and the neighbors were more than happy to oblige. They threw handfuls of candy into Nicki's bag and told her to come back again on her way home. She went after candy like never before.

She came home with almost fifteen pounds of candy, and I came home forty dollars lighter.

She was motivated because she had a new goal. She wasn't just going after candy, she was on a mission, a mission to set a new candy-collection record.

Occasional rewards can be used to motivate, and also to help us face something unpleasant.

Recently Dani needed to get a blood test. It was a needle-in-the-arm type of blood test, so naturally she wasn't looking forward to it. I told her if she was good, we'd go shopping for a treat afterward. She did amazingly well and got through the test with just a few tears.

I told her how proud I was of her and said, "That wasn't too bad, was it Dani?" She took a deep breath and said, "Mom . . . two words . . . Toys "R" Us."

We all have little rewards that really motivate us. Make a promise to yourself that after you reach your next business milestone you'll treat yourself to something special. Whether it's a trip to the salon or to the toy store, make it something that is special, just for you. You deserve it.

If you feel like you're in a rut with your business, try setting a new goal for yourself. Make it something concrete, like a dollar sales amount or a new traffic level for your Web site. Write down how you're going to reach your goal and schedule a realistic time frame in which to accomplish it.

To keep yourself on track, set up a weekly meeting with yourself or with another work-at-home mom. See if you're on schedule to reach your goal and decide if you need to make adjustments.

Another great idea is to keep a working journal. Write about what you've accomplished and how you've achieved it. You might include both your home and business life. Writing our thoughts on paper often helps to clarify ideas and solutions.

Now that you have your goal and a plan to reach it, you need incentive. When we're working by ourselves, we don't receive the typical awards often used as incentives in the traditional workplace. Why not buy yourself a gift certificate? Choose your favorite store, buy a certificate, write "Congratulations!" on the envelope, and put it away until you reach your goal.

Melissa Duquette, founder of StampFolk.com, says the best gift she can receive is a gift certificate to the office supply store—something that others moms don't always understand. She says, "I was sitting with some moms at my daughter's dance class. One of them was looking through a jewelry catalog, commenting that she would have to leave the catalog out for her husband so he could pick out her Christmas gifts. I said, 'I'd be happy if my husband bought all my presents at Staples.' She turned to me and said, 'You poor thing.' I just laughed. My husband knows if he really wants to make me happy, he should shop for me at the office supply store."

I've bought a gift certificate for myself in the past, and it's a lot of fun. Plus, it will give you a chance to do a little extra networking when you cash in your gift certificate and your salesperson asks what occasion you're celebrating. You never know when you'll run into a new customer.

BE THE BUNNY

You know that special time of year? Chocolate is hidden, candy is tucked away in drawers and cupboards. . . . No, I'm not talking about the preswimsuit dieting season, I'm talking about Easter time! Whatever traditions and beliefs your family has, I'm guessing that you participate in some type of deception with your children from time to time throughout the year.

I used to be troubled by this. I wondered if all the tricks and deceptions would have some long-lasting negative effects on my daughter, something that she would have to talk to her therapist about years from now. Then all her problems would be summed up in one sentence, "It's all your mom's fault."

To counter this, I tried to help distinguish fact from fiction. We played "real or pretend," where I mentioned a character and she said "real" or "pretend." One day I asked her, "Tooth fairy, real or pretend?" She rolled her eyes and said, "Oh, I know that one, Mom. It's just a guy dressed up like a fairy."

Of course this wasn't true, unless Mike was up to something I wasn't aware of. Then we would all have to see a therapist. That response made me decide to quit playing "real or pretend" with her.

She obviously still wanted to believe that fairies exchange money for teeth and giant bunnies hide chocolate eggs. I decided to enjoy the innocence of her childhood for as long as I could, and I have to admit that I really like playing my role in these traditions too. But why does it have to be limited to special occasions?

I figure, why not spread a little magic every day? Anonymously send coffee and doughnuts to a customer's office; hide a dollar in the sand at the playground; send flowers to those ladies at the coffee shop who greet you cheerfully after you've been up all night working on a project (and probably look like it!). Bring chocolate eggs to the workers at the copy center who finished that rush job for you ahead of time. Surprise the postman with a treat. I'm sure you are in contact with many people every day, those who could use a lift and those who help make your day a little easier. The treats and surprises don't have to be expensive, and you'll find that it's a lot of fun for you too.

And I benefit too. I realize that I have more energy to devote to my business and I'm more motivated in general when I spread the joy around.

Give it a try today—be the bunny!

BIG, BIGGER, BIGGEST

There's a trend within my peer group to drive bigger and bigger vehicles. It is not unusual to see a caravan of trucks lined up each morning, heading down the road to school. It's reminiscent of Smokey and the Bandit. All we have to do is give everyone a CB and a handle, and we got us a convoy!

Do you feel the bigger-is-better pressure in your home business? Do you feel you have to continue to grow to be successful? Do you feel like you're not giving your all to your business unless you take on every project that comes your way?

I have a secret for work-at-home moms: bigger isn't necessarily better. I know you may not read this advice in business magazines or books, but we work-at-home moms are already breaking the traditional business rules anyway.

If you are starting to feel stressed, like you're being pulled in too many directions at once, I say it's time to take a break. Take a moment, step back, and rethink your priorities. You may find that it's time to say, "I don't need more right now." Recognize when it's time to say no to a new project. Sometimes good enough is good enough.

If you're happy with the income you're making, your current workload, and the hours you devote to your business, leave well enough alone. You have to consider what expanding could mean to the time that you have to spend with your family, your children and your husband.

So remember, bigger isn't always better. Heck, even Pamela Lee had her implants removed.

I Need Sleep

I'm often asked how I manage to fit everything into my schedule. Taking care of a home and family is a full-time job in itself. Add a home business to the mix, and something's got to give. The main thing that's "given" for me is sleep. I don't get much. Every time I turn around there's another sleep study in the paper. I read that sleep deprivation will make me fat. Then I read that people who sleep less than eight hours a night live longer. Great, so I'll live to be an old lady, a *fat* old lady.

Since I'm staying home so that I'm able to spend more time with my kids, it would defeat the purpose to be working all the time when I'm here with them. So I've had to be a little creative as far as when I fit my work into my daily schedule. I usually wake up well before the rest of the house, and in this way I'm able to put in several hours of work before anyone else even wakes up.

Once one has a baby, one gives up any thought of really sleeping soundly ever again anyway. When I was a child and there was a sound in the night, I knew someone else would take care of it. Now if something happens in the night, I know that I'm responsible. Every little groan and creak in the house wakes me up.

It seems that I'm always up in the middle of the night. One night Dani called for me—by the way, one of the sweetest things a mother can hear in the middle of the night is her child call out "Daddy!" But the other night she called for me, just to tell me, "Mom, if you take one letter out of *planet* you get *plant*. So someone could think that Mars wasn't the red planet but the red plant."

"Right . . . Dani, next time when you wake up thinking about something like this, ask yourself if Mommy really needs to hear it right now, or if it can wait until morning."

"Oh, I did, Mom, I knew you'd want to hear it right away."

How could I argue with that? She fell back asleep and I was up at 5:00 A.M.

I really have to discipline myself to work when I have the chance. This isn't like an office in a building downtown, which has a cleaning crew come through every night to empty the trash and vacuum. If I've left something out the night before, it's still there in the morning. It can be stressful.

I've tested several stress-reducing methods myself. I gave medi-

YOU'VE GOT A

HOME BUSINESS

YOU'VE GOT   YOU'VE GOT

KIDS   BILLS

got coffee?

tation a try; I fell asleep. I don't know how Michelangelo ever paint-
ed the ceiling of the Sistine Chapel. He must have been really well
rested, because I fall asleep every time I get horizontal. I crawled
under our dining room table to tighten some screws one night and I
fell asleep. The kids just left me there.

Mike came home and asked, "Where's Mom?"

"She's sleeping under the table," they told him.

"Oh," he said. Like that was normal.

I didn't wake up until the next morning.

"Weren't you worried about me?" I asked my husband when I
woke up.

"I figured you needed the rest," he said.

"Thanks for being so thoughtful, honey."

One morning I was so tired, I got into the shower and stood
there for a while, thinking something was wrong but not quite sure
what, when I realized that I was still wearing my underwear. I suppose it was kind of like doing the laundry and cleaning myself at the
same time. I'm all for multitasking, but that was a bit much.

The trick is learning to recognize when we need to recharge our
batteries before we hit the wall. I now try to pay a little more attention to my body and make sure that I'm getting rest and taking care
of myself—and I leave doing the laundry for the laundry room.

REPORT CARD TIME

We all know them—mothers who display their children's awards, test
scores, and report cards like mounted hunting trophies on their walls
and refrigerators. Our kids need to know we're proud of them, but I
say we mothers deserve some recognition too. Something more than
just a Sunday in May when we receive a card and a potted petunia,
please.

THE MOMMY WARS

Just now it's report card time again. How long has it been since you received a report card?

If you're working at home, you are probably dealing with many challenges. Business issues, deadlines, and lean times. Family issues, from nonsupportive husbands to sick kids and family squabbles.

But you've kept at it. You are the one who is with your children all day, and you know better than anyone else does what is best for them. You've dealt with the criticism and complaints. You've been there when your kids needed you, and you're building a business at the same time. You are the model for the new workplace, the mothers of the future.

It's about time you received a little recognition. Give yourself a pat on the back. Print out the great e-mails or reviews you've received, reread the notes your kids have written to you. Gather them in a scrapbook that you can take out when you need a pick-me-up. Think about all your accomplishments: your business success, the money you've saved, the time you've spent with your family. Better yet, give yourself a report card. Give yourself a big A+. Take down one of two of the kids' pictures and hang your report card on the refrigerator. The kids won't mind and you deserve it.

PROBLEM
I'm lonely! I miss my coworkers and adult conversation.

SOLUTIONS FROM SISTER ZOOS
So am I! Let's have lunch! No, really, this is a common problem. We are kind of isolated. Find a moms' group in your area, or start one. I'm active in my church, and most of my friends are from church. But it still gets lonely sometimes.

Jamie R., Florida

Network! WAHM.com is the real deal when it comes to conversations with other adults.

Calissa L., Florida

Because promoting your home-based business is integral to your success, use that time to reestablish old connections and forge new ones. Former coworkers and employers make an invaluable pool for networking opportunities. Take them to lunch—while taking advantage of a much-needed tax write-off—and talk about your new business. Chances are, they'll know someone who knows someone who needs your expertise.

Mikalee D., Nevada

We all miss our coworkers when we first leave our jobs. We spend our entire days around certain groups of people who seem to leave our lives when we become stay-at-home or work-at-home moms. Get involved in a church Bible study or a mommy-and-me program at your local park-and-rec, start a small group at home where you can all work on a hobby while chatting, meet with other stay-at-home moms once a week at a local park or take turns at each other's homes. During the rest of the week, you can network online.

Alyice E., Wisconsin

Schedule regular outings that you look forward to every week. Arrange to go out by yourself or with your husband. My escape from the home office is movies. I go to movies every week, and I always come home fresh with new ideas, ready to go to work again. I also go to our neighborhood restaurant and sit at the family-style bar to have a salad and chat with people. It doesn't take long to get to know the regulars who also get out to enjoy a meal and conversations. Your escape can be a bowling night, meeting your spouse for an early dinner, going to the park to walk. I know online business associates who don't get out very much, and the difference in our attitudes is tremendous. Make getting out a priority.

Alanna W., Oklahoma

Get online fast! Find a chat room or bulletin board you're comfortable with, and go for it—now. If you're not housebound, get out to book readings and cafés, but don't make the situation worse by doing nothing. If you're a new mom, get to a mommy-and-me group, play groups, park, anything . . . but get out!

Rose Marie B., New York

This is almost the last chapter, but taking care of yourself shouldn't be the last thing you consider. Be sure to take a break from time to time, nurture your friendships, and keep up with your hobbies. These little sanity breaks will keep you happy and motivated.

12

Some Final Thoughts

My Dream Life

Several weeks ago I was up in the middle of the night with Dani. She was sick and hadn't quite made it to the bathroom, if you know what I mean. As soon as I got that cleaned up, she got a bloody nose. Our new puppy took advantage of my inattention and relieved herself all over the kitchen. That's when I noticed the ants. They had set up a multilane ant expressway in the kitchen and were all having a party on my countertops. It was 4:00 A.M. by the time I got everything cleaned up. It was like an old Johnny Carson Carnac the Magnificent joke:

Answer: Vomit, poop, urine, ants, and blood.

Question: What did I clean up last night?

Since I wasn't going to be able to sleep anyway, I figured I might as well get some work done. I sat down at my computer. The first e-mail I opened said: "Cheryl, you're living my *dream!*"

I'd hate to see her nightmare.

But the funny thing is, it's my dream too.

Each year as we prepare for the holidays, I dream of a beautifully decorated house, with the scents of freshly baked apple pie, happy family members joyously stringing popcorn, and crackling fires. The reality, however, is always another story.

Maybe this year, I think, we will have a Martha Stewart holiday. We'll make garlands from fresh evergreen boughs. Our Christmas tree will have a unified theme and color scheme, we'll go to the ballet, our pies and whipped toppings will be made from scratch, wassail will waft through the house (if I can figure out what wassail and wafting are), the stuffing will be made with roasted garlic and sausage. No Stove Top this year!

So I start to unpack the ornaments. I pull out the little Baby Jesus in a Walnut Shell that Nicki made when she was in kindergarten. Next I find the homemade reindeer, his antlers made from tracing her little hands. I put them back in the box; there's no room for these decorations in my "perfect holiday" vision.

At church the children are practicing for the annual Christmas pageant. The youngest baby Jesus we can find is ten months old, Mary is allergic to the hay, the shepherds are fighting over who gets to carry the biggest stick. The wise men are wearing bathrobes for their costumes. This is not a high-class *Nutcracker* ballet production.

But then I think about the kind of holiday we would have without these things that have become traditions in our family. The vision looks beautiful, but it feels empty. I imagine we could do the fantasy holiday if we really wanted to, but how I would miss that handprint reindeer hanging on the wall. I want to watch the kids at church perform the Christmas story. Yes, most of our decorations do consist of glued macaroni and walnut shells. These things might not fit the vision of a perfect holiday season, but they're my vision of how the holidays should be.

So bring on the Stove Top and Cool Whip; I don't want to change a thing.

Cleaning up after ants, dogs, and children at 4:00 A.M. may not be what twenty-two-year-old Cheryl had envisioned for her future as a successful businesswoman either, but now that I'm living my dream, I realize how wrong she was.

I know there are thousands of other moms who have chosen the home business lifestyle too. I see them with their preschoolers at the office supply store. We meet online, and we chat in the middle of the night at the copy center.

Now it's time for *you* to take action and live *your* dream. You won't regret it.

Resources

BOOKS

101 Best Home-based Businesses for Women
Priscilla Y. Huff
Prima Publishing, 2002

Cashflow Quadrant: Rich Dad's Guide to Financial Freedom
Robert T. Kiyosaki, Sharon L. Lechter
Warner Books, 2000

The Entrepreneurial Parent: How to Earn Your Living from Home and Still Enjoy Your Family, Your Life, and Your Work
Paul Edwards, Lisa M. Roberts, Sarah Edwards
J. P. Tarcher, 2002

Investing 101
Kathy Kristof
Bloomberg Press, 2000

Home-Based Business for Dummies
Paul Edwards, Sarah Edwards, Peter Economy
John Wiley & Sons, 2000

Home Comforts: The Art and Science of Keeping House
Cheryl Mendelson
Scribner, 1999

Home Management 101: A Guide for Busy Parents
Debbie Williams
Champion Press, 2001

Mompreneurs: A Mother's Practical Step-By-Step Guide to Work-at-Home Success
Ellen H. Parlapiano, Patricia Cobe
Berkeley Publishing Group, 1996

Mompreneurs Online: Using the Internet to Build Work at Home Success
Patricia Cobe, Ellen H. Parlapiano
Perigee, 2001

Organizing from the Inside Out
Julie Morgenstern
Owl Books, 1998

Rich Dad, Poor Dad: What the Rich Teach Their Kids about Money—That the Poor and Middle Class Do Not!
Robert T. Kiyosaki, Sharon L. Lechter
Warner Books, 2000

Stay-at-Home Handbook
Cheryl Gochnauer
Intervarsity Press, 2002

The Stay-at-Home Mom's Guide to Making Money from Home: Choosing the Business That's Right for You Using the Skills and Interests You Already Have
Liz Folger
Prima Publishing, 2000

WEB SITES

Work-at-Home/Business Sites

WAHM.com—The Online Magazine for Work-at-Home Moms
http://www.wahm.com
http://www.wahm.com/states.html
The second address has links to all the U.S. states' business regulations pages.

Bizy Moms
http://www.bizymoms.com

Direct Selling Association
http://www.dsa.org
(Includes a directory of direct-sales companies)

Entrepreneur Magazine
http://www.entrepreneur.com

The Entrepreneurial Parent
http://www.en-parent.com/

Home-Based Working Moms
http://www.hbwm.com

IRS Online
http://www.irs.gov

Moms Network
http://www.momsnetwork.com

Service Corps of Retired Executives
http://www.score.org

U.S. Small Business Administration
http://www.sba.gov

Family, Parenting, and Other Helpful Web Sites

20ish Parents
http://www.20ishparents.com

Baby Corner
http://www.thebabycorner.com/

Baby University
http://www.babyuniversity.com/

Chef Mom
http://www.chefmom.com

ChildFun
http://www.childfun.com

ePregnancy
http://www.epregnancy.com

Fabulous Foods
http://www.fabulousfoods.com

FamilyCorner.com Magazine
http://www.familycorner.com

Fly Lady (home cleaning and organizing tips)
http://www.flylady.net

Frugal Moms
http://www.frugalmoms.com

GeoParent
http://www.geoparent.com

Holiday Cookies
http://www.holidaycookies.com

Idea Marketers (source of content online)
http://www.ideamarketers.com

Lazy Gourmets
http://www.lazygourmets.com

Main Street Mom
http://www.mainstreetmom.com

Myria (site for moms)
http://www.myria.com

Old Fashioned Living
http://www.oldfashionedliving.com

Organized Times
http://www.organizedtimes.com

Parenting Humor
http://www.parentinghumor.com

Parenting Toolbox
http://www.parentingtoolbox.com

The Second Wives Club (stepparenting help)
http://www.secondwivesclub.com

Index

TALKING MONEY
Everything You Need to Know about Your
Finances and Your Future

by Jean Chatzky

Today everyone is talking about money: how to spend it, how to save it, and how to invest it. But how much of this wall-to-wall money talk really makes sense? And how does all of it affect you? Now *Today Show* financial expert and MONEY magazine columnist Jean Chatzky brings her down-to-earth style to a book for real people with real issues about money. In this amazingly concise and easy-to-understand guide, she tells you what you need to know about all money matters. So grab a cup of coffee, pull up a chair, and start . . . *Talking Money*.

"When it comes to your personal finances, Jean Chatzky tells you exactly what you need to know—in language you can understand!"
—Katie Couric, coanchor of
NBC News Today